CURING &
SMOKING
MADE AT HOME

A FIREFLY BOOK

Published by Firefly Books Ltd. 2012

Copyright © 2012 Octopus Publishing Group Ltd
Text copyright © 2012 Dick and James Strawbridge,
Jera Enterprises Ltd

First printing

Publisher Cataloging-in-Publication Data (U.S.)

Strawbridge, Dick.
    Curing & smoking : made at home / Dick and James
Strawbridge.
[176] p. : col. photos. ; cm.
Includes index.
Summary: An introduction to the art of curing and
smoking foods, equipment needed and recipes using
the final products.
ISBN-13: 978-1-77085-077-4 (pbk.)
1. Food – Preservation. 2. Smoked foods. 3. Cooking
(Smoked foods). I. Strawbridge, James. II. Curing and
smoking. III. Title.
641.46 dc23   TX609.S763 2012

Library and Archives Canada Cataloguing in Publication

Strawbridge, Dick
    Curing & smoking: made at home / Dick & James
Strawbridge.
Includes index.
ISBN 978-1-77085-077-4
    1. Smoked foods. 2. Cooking (Smoked foods). 3.
Food—Preservation. I. Strawbridge, James II. Title.
III. Title: Curing and smoking.
TX609.S77 2012   641.4'6   C2012-900387-5

Published in the United States by
Firefly Books (U.S.) Inc.
P.O. Box 1338, Ellicott Station
Buffalo, New York 14205

Published in Canada by
Firefly Books Ltd.
66 Leek Crescent
Richmond Hill, Ontario L4B 1H1

Photography by Nick Pope

Printed and bound in China

Curing & Smoking was developed, designed and
conceived by Mitchell Beazley, an imprint of Octopus
Publishing Group Limited, Endeavour House, 189
Shaftesbury Avenue, London, WC2H 8JY

Neither the authors nor the publishers take any
responsibility for any injury or damage resulting from
the use of techniques shown or described in this book.

Both metric and imperial measurements are given
for the recipes. Use one set of measures only, not a
mixture of both. Quantities for most dry ingredients
are listed by weight, since this provides greater
precision. However, approximate quantities by volume
are also listed.

Ovens should be preheated to the specified
temperature. If using a convection oven, follow the
manufacturer's instructions for adjusting the time and
temperature. Grills should also be preheated.

This book includes dishes made with nuts and nut
derivatives and those who may be potentially
vulnerable to these allergies, such as pregnant
and nursing mothers, the sick, the elderly, babies
and children, to avoid dishes made with nuts and
nut oils. It is also prudent to check the labels of
prepared ingredients for the possible inclusion of nut
derivatives.

The U.S. Food and Drug Administration and Health
Canada advise that eggs should not be consumed
raw. This book contains some dishes made with raw or
lightly cooked eggs. It is prudent for more vulnerable
people, such as pregnant and nursing mothers, the sick,
the elderly, babies and young children, to avoid dishes
made with uncooked or lightly cooked eggs.

Thank you to everyone who has
taken the time to teach us so that
we can now pass it on to Indy and
anyone else who will listen.

CURING & SMOKING
Made at Home

Dick & James
Strawbridge

FIREFLY BOOKS

CONTENTS

INTRODUCTION

Whether you wish to find ways to preserve your excess produce, save money or just make something delicious, learning how to cure and smoke your own food is great fun. This book explains what is possible and offers encouragement: we want to give you the confidence and knowledge to gather the necessary materials and start experimenting with ingredients you may well already have in your fridge and pantry.

THE BENEFITS OF CURING & SMOKING

Cured and smoked foods, with their distinctive flavors and textures, are part of our history, and in the days before supermarkets offered fresh food seven days a week, these preserving methods were essentials skills. So why try smoking and curing food today? Preparing smoked and cured food at home is not always cheaper than buying it from a store (although it frequently can be), but the satisfaction alone is a good enough reason -- the pride you feel putting your own cured produce on the table for your family and friends to enjoy is immense. What you produce will not taste exactly the same as the mass-produced equivalent; it will be unique and truly amazing. Our main motivation is the quality of the food we make.

It all starts with the raw ingredients. The humble salami, for example, is nothing more than pork meat, fat, flavorings and salt. Given the amount of effort you put in and the time it takes for the product to mature, it seems counterproductive to use anything other than the best ingredients you can possibly source. (For us that means rearing our own organic pigs -- it's an awful lot easier to buy the pork from a good butcher, but anyone who has reared their own pigs will understand the satisfaction we feel.) Keeping it simple allows the essence of the food to come through. Be in no doubt that any added "flavoring" on a food label should set off warning bells -- does "apple woodsmoke flavoring" mean that a piece of meat or cheese has been smoked in apple wood? Sadly not; it will probably have been rubbed in a smoky-tasting, orange-coloured chemical.

Just because society has moved on from a rural-based, agricultural society and most of us now congregate in towns and cities doesn't mean we can't produce our own food. Anyone with even the smallest kitchen or yard can do a surprising amount of curing and smoking. We've been smoking cheeses and curing meats and fish for more than 20 years in modestly sized spaces, and it was only when we moved to our small farm in 2005 that we started rearing our own meat. By that stage, we had honed our skills and had acquired the confidence to try anything and everything.

WHERE TO START

This book will encourage you to try all facets of curing and smoking to see what you enjoy. We show you all the key methods, as well as give you ideas and recipes so that you can make a dish with your products as the star. Keeping food for long periods does require a degree of common sense, so we point out where you should take care and when to be cautious. Once you have mastered the principles, treat the methods and recipes as guides and experiment.

Before you launch into one of the projects, it is worth taking stock of what you are trying to achieve. Quality, cost, flavor and availability are all valid motivators: our initial attempts at cold smoking came about because smoked cheeses were both expensive and difficult to find. Today they are much more plentiful, but the quality still leaves a lot to be desired. We love the fact that we can make a batch of smoked cheese -- we can do up to 10 kg (22 lbs) at a time -- for the cost of the cheese and a bucket of sawdust (usually that's free, but it's only fair to give the carpenter who gave it to us some home-made product in return). Rather than using a very basic cheese, as most commercially produced smoked cheese tends to be, we buy local mature cheeses when they are on sale or use a specialty cheese that takes our fancy. We also control the type of smoke we use to smoke it and exactly how smoky we make the finished product. As we have all these variables in our control we are able to make a unique product that is special to us -- when was the last time you saw a beech-smoked Stilton or a chestnut-smoked Brie in a store? They are both great, by the way, especially with a slice of nice, crisp apple. We also love hot-smoked chicken in salads, but had problems finding it. That was all the incentive we needed to learn about hot smoking, and now we can have organic hot-smoked chicken whenever we want.

CREATING SOMETHING SPECIAL

The pork we rear is of the highest quality and relatively expensive, as our pigs are much older than most that are reared commercially. For purely commercial reasons, farmed pigs are kept for the period of maximum growth and then slaughtered. Our pigs, however, are slowly grown and each piece of meat has taken a lot of effort. We could fill our freezer with meat, use each piece carefully and savor every mouthful, but we like to find a way to add value. When we cure or smoke our meat the resulting product is worth a lot more -- for example, an air-dried leg of pork is about five times the price of a fresh leg of pork. So the air-dried pork we eat would have cost us a small fortune had we not made it ourselves. If you are not rearing your own meat then find a good independent butcher. You can follow recommendations, but it's worth going in and having a chat -- though it's best to try to avoid a busy Saturday if you want to spend some time understanding how the butcher's meat is sourced.

Traditionally, people had a well-stocked pantry and cellar to see them through the lean winter months. While few people are motivated to cure and smoke by the thought of having no food in the short, dark winter days, having your own stores does give you the flexibility of harvesting and gathering food when it is readily available and in season. There is, of course, the slight problem of having a large enough storage space, so before you turn into a curing and smoking demon, it's best to make sure that you have somewhere to store your hard work. As well as being a talking point over dinner, the homemade food you have put such effort into will be a treat for those who are constrained by what they can buy in the stores.

Flicking through this book, you will, we hope, have seen photographs of food you know you would enjoy, but you may not be convinced that you are capable of making it. You are! There is nothing in this book that is not completely achievable. We believe you will find curing and smoking your own food as rewarding, as enjoyable and, above all, as delicious as we do. It's just a matter of having the desire to give it a try.

Dick & James

CURE & SMOKE

When you set out to learn any new skill, you are faced with
a mind-boggling number of choices. The main problem can be
deciding when -- and where -- to begin. Most of the projects in
this book can be started very quickly. You may need to take a
shopping trip for some raw materials, but you will probably be
able to get your hands on enough ingredients that are already in
your kitchen to try something right away.

WHAT METHOD TO TRY FIRST

We suggest that you start by making
what you love the most or what you
cannot find in stores. If you have ever
been disappointed by "premium" quality
bacon that when grilled, lacked any flavor
other than saltiness, do something about
it. If you find the white residue that is
released into the pan when you cook
your cured meat a little worrying, take
charge of your own destiny and make
your own. We started with smoking
cheese simply because we loved it and
good smoked cheese was hard to find.

BRINING

Curing meat is an ancient skill, and
brining is the most widely practiced
and fundamental of the methods. This
wet cure is very forgiving and requires
very little specialist equipment: a food-
grade plastic container is all you need
to get started. You will need some space
in the fridge for your container of brine
or at the very least a cool storage space.

Try a basic cure first, and then you can
go on to vary the ingredients. If at first
you do succeed, don't be fooled into
thinking you have mastered the art:
you are immediately faced with lots of
decisions. Do you make the same cure
again to show how clever you are? Do
you change the cut of meat and keep
the same method. Do you vary the cure
and add your own aromatics? There is
no right answer, but the fun lies in the
experimenting. Keep a notebook, and as
well as writing down the date and details
of what you did, make some tasting
notes. It's surprisingly easy to forget
which of your many delectable dishes
was your favourite.

DRY CURING

Dry curing can be a method in its own
right, or the forerunner to air drying or
smoking. The container required for dry
curing can be as simple as a crock or
other large pot or a plastic food container.
Using a hardwood box or barrel is the

ultimate in traditional dry curing, and such items are sometimes available to buy, but you should start by using a simple tub instead. If you pop a couple of extra items into your cart next time you are in the supermarket you will be able to start dry curing the moment you get back home.

Making gravlax was one of our first forays into dry curing, which involved making a press (page 57), although you can improvise one. One day a side of salmon was on offer at the fish market and, having bought it, we decided to "add value," as gravlax is probably three or four times the price of fresh fish. If we are completely honest, the press has never really saved us money, as we tend to eat a lot more of this delicious dish than most families. Not that we are complaining.

AIR DRYING

Most people love the idea of air drying meat – imagine having hams in the attic or salami and chorizo in a coldroom – but trying to determine the perfect location for their maturing products can stop them from trying. It is worth remembering that there is more to air drying than legs of meat hanging up for all to see – air-dried foods range from bunches of herbs to beef jerky. By all means start by hanging up your excess chillies to dry in the kitchen, but there is something special about curing meat. You do not need special equipment to make salami, but this method does require some patience because the meat takes time to mature as it dries out. You might as well be patient in the preparation, too: equipment can be expensive if you go out and buy it immediately,

but hand-operated meat grinders or sausage machines come up for sale on the internet or in the classified ads in the paper. Keep your eyes open and think ahead to improve your chances of spotting a bargain. And you can always improvise – we have made some very acceptable sausages on board a boat using a bicycle pump.

HOT SMOKING

With hot-smoked goods widely available in delis and supermarkets, you will already know if you like the flavors before you even make your first batch. Be prepared to be very pleased with yourself – "made at home" is always better than "store bought!" There are a number of rules to follow when hot smoking, so take the time to read about how to do it properly: at certain temperatures,

microbes and bacteria can grow to dangerous levels (see pages 98 and 105 for more detailed information). A stovetop smoker is the usual place to start, as it is all but foolproof and can be improvised from items found in most kitchens. That said, with some rudimentary DIY skills you can build an impressive smoker that offers plenty of flexibility and allows you to expand your repertoire of smoked foods. Commercially produced domestic hot-smokers are readily available on the internet. If you are not keen on DIY, they are a functional, reliable solution.

COLD SMOKING

We have worn out several cold-smokers. Ours have always been based on oil drums, but any container that holds smoke for long enough to infuse your food will work. Cold smoking is probably one of the easiest ways to produce very tasty food that will surprise those around you, and as long as your chosen smoking box does not get warm enough to allow bacteria to grow, you will succeed. Before you begin, you will need to source some sawdust and wood shavings. Make sure they are pure apple wood or oak or whichever type of wood you prefer, otherwise you will fail to get the wood's typical characteristics and flavors. Half a bucketful is more than enough for one batch, but it's best to source sacks so you can repeat and experiment with flavors. It is worth having a collection of different sawdusts so you can present a platter of flavors. Make sure you let people know you need the sawdust or shavings to smoke food because they will be interested and well disposed toward you. Letting them try your products will stand you in good stead in the future.

EQUIPPING YOURSELF

We don't like spending a lot of money on our equipment, but we do like good-quality items that will last a long time. If you decide you are going to make your own curing box or smoker, take the time to make something that does exactly what you want it to – not only is that satisfying in itself, but it will also become a family heirloom. It is also worth keeping your eyes peeled for second-hand equipment, but make sure the items are functional and not those that have been treated to make them attractive. If you know anyone else who cures or smokes food it is always worth asking them for advice, as most people are happy to share their ideas and experiences.

1

BRINING

INTRODUCTION TO
BRINING

Brining is one of the most effective ways to preserve food. The great thing about this method is that it keeps the meat or fish moist, perfect for use in a variety of dishes. Adding strong flavors with a selection of herbs and spices to a saline solution allows them to really penetrate the meat or fish and enhance the taste. Brining takes a long time to do -- normally 24 hours or more, so plan ahead and be patient. It'll be worth the wait!

HOW BRINING WORKS

Brining is a simple process. Meat is soaked in a mixture of water and curing agents and becomes tender and stays moist. The salt not only breaks down tough muscle fibers but also interacts with the proteins in the meat so that the cells draw and retain the brine.

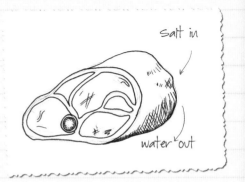

salt in

water out

GUIDELINES

- Use 500 g (1 pound) of salt (about 500 ml/2 cups) for every 5 L (5 quarts) of water.
- Use at least 50% brine to meat; for example, 1 kg (2 pounds) of meat will need a minimum of 500 ml (2 cups) of brine.
- To brine, use either a bag or a container that is about the same dimensions as the meat, adding more brine if necessary to immerse the meat.
- Always use at least the advised percentage of salt in the saline solution.
- Change the solution regularly if you are curing a large cut of meat.
- Always keep your food submerged and properly refrigerated, below 5°C (41°F).
- Never reuse a brine solution.

THE BRINE SOLUTION

You need salt and water to brine food. You can use any type of salt: table salt is inexpensive and easy to come by, while kosher salt has a cleaner flavor and dissolves more easily. Generally, brining is achieved with a large proportion of salt and a little sugar. However, you will find that some recipes require you to carry out a sweet brine cure after the initial brining (for example, see pastrami, pages 108–109). This is because sugar can also be a great way to cure meat and fish if it is used in the right proportion. Not only does sugar help with reducing the salty flavors, but it also increases the growth of lactobacillus – a bacteria beneficial to the curing process.

TESTING THE BRINE

If you have a salinometer you can precisely measure the saltiness of your brine. As a rule,

Little does she know what's in store for her

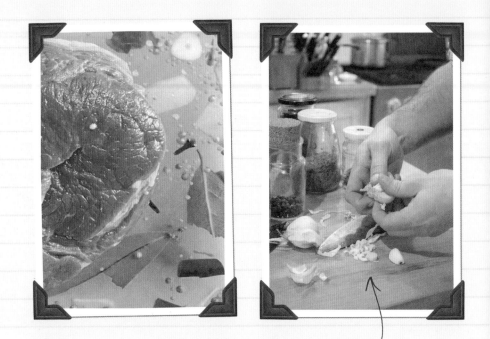

Natural flavors and no added colorings

the best brine strengths for different types of meat are:

- chicken – 40%
- bacon loins – 60%
- hams, shoulders – 60–80%
- fish – 80%

These figures are based on a simple salt and water solution. If you add sugar, the brine will be more dense. If you want a stronger solution add more salt, and if you need a weaker brine add more water. Keep in mind that a salinometer measures the density of a solution containing salt and water. Adding other ingredients to your brine may alter the density of the solution, so always test the brine before you add any flavorings.

BRINE FLAVORINGS

You can add flavor to your brine with herbs and spices. A traditional cure mix could include:

Bay leaves

Cloves

Juniper berries

Ginger

Coriander seeds

Black peppercorns

Rosemary

Thyme

Garlic

Star anise

BRINE CONTAINERS

You will need a container in which to seal the solution and the meat for a period of time. A freezer bag laid on a tray can work well for small quantities. The bigger the piece of meat, the bigger the container, and for a leg of ham you may need a very large one, such as a cooler.

RECORD-KEEPING

Always clearly label meats that are curing, as the last thing you want is to waste meat because it cures for too long or not long enough. Keep a notebook and record which brines and flavorings you have used and which ones were your favourites.

BRINE SOLUTIONS AND TIMING

PRODUCT	WATER	SALT	SUGAR	TIME
LARGE CUT e.g. beef brisket	5 L (5 quarts)	1.5 kg (3 pounds)	500 g (1 pound) (about 625 ml/ 2½ cups)	3–5 days
MEDIUM CUT e.g. pork chops	500 ml (2 cups)	50 g (2 ounces) (about 60 ml/¼ cup)	50 g (2 ounces)	48 hours
SWEET CURE e.g. ham	5 L (5 quarts)	500 g (1 pound)	750 g (1½ pounds)	24 hours

Pork loin turned into a delicious ham

METHOD #1

BRINED PORK

Taking raw meat or fish and altering its texture, taste and quality is a magical thing to try at home. We are always pleasantly surprised at how you can take a large lump of pork and transform it into a moist, tasty ham. There is a common misconception that ham is a cut of pork. In fact, ham is simply a leg of pork that has been cured, and brining is the key. You can also brine other cuts of pork to maximize the flavor, and even fish such as herring.

PREPARING THE SOLUTION

The most important part of brining is to get the saline solution right. For a large fresh ham with the bone in, mix 5 L (5 quarts) of hot water with 500 g (1 pound) each of salt (about 2 cups/500 ml) and sugar (about 2½ cups/625 ml) in a large plastic container. Stir to dissolve then allow to cool. This is the essential part of your brining process, so make sure you get it right! The stronger the brine, the faster the curing time, and the larger the meat, the more brining it will need.

ADDING THE FLAVOR

A ham that has been cured simply in brine can be tasty – especially if you have chosen pork from a well-reared rare-breed pig. However, part of the alchemy involved in brining depends on herbs and spices. These flavors will infuse the meat with intense depth as the brine draws out the moisture. The salt and sugar preserve the meat, while the herbs and spices add depth of flavor. Drop the flavorings directly into the brine or tie them up in a small cheesecloth bag.

CURING YOUR PORK

You will need a brining container with a lid or a resealable bag. The container should be the same dimensions as the meat you are curing.

Pour the brine into the container and add your cut of pork, making sure that the meat is fully immersed. Put a lid on the container and refrigerate for 3–4 days. Turn the meat every day – morning and evening if you can – so that you achieve an even cure. Finally, remove the meat from the brine, rinse under a running tap and pat dry with papertowels. Now you've got a delicious ham, ready to cook.

If you are curing a really large cut of meat that won't fit in the fridge, try using a food-grade cooler with some ice packs in it. The ice packs will need refreshing regularly in order to make sure that the meat stays cool enough, but it's a great way to deal with bigger cuts of meat.

INJECTING A LARGER CUT OF MEAT

Large cuts of meat can benefit from having the brine solution injected into the deeper parts. A brining syringe is useful for speeding up curing times, placing the brine near the bone in the middle of the piece of meat for added flavor and a speedier cure.

NOW TRY: BACON

Making home-cured bacon is easy. Cure it in the same way as a cut of ham, but add more salt to speed up the process. For a 3 kg (6½-pound) piece of pork, use 1 kg (2 pounds) of salt (about 1 L/4 cups) and 350 g (11½ ounces) of sugar (about 1¾ cups/425 ml) to 5 L (5 quarts) of water and cure for 24 hours. If a cool space is available, hang the "green" bacon for a day before placing it in the fridge for storage. It will keep for about 2 weeks or even longer if you smoke it (see pages 142–143).

A FLAVORED BRINE FOR PORK

For 4 kg (9 pounds) of pork

500 g (1 pound) salt (about 500 ml/2 cups)
200 g (7 ounces) sugar (about 250 ml/1 cup)
5 L (5 quarts) water
4 bay leaves
1 large onion, cut in half
10 garlic cloves
2 stalks celery, roughly chopped
5 ml (1 teaspoon) mustard seeds
5 whole cloves
5 ml (1 teaspoon) chili flakes
2 allspice berries
5 ml (1 teaspoon) peppercorns

HOW TO BRINE A PORK BELLY

1 Place the pork in a glass container. Pour in the water and then add the salt and the rest of the ingredients for the flavored brine.

2 Add the pork to the brine solution, cover and refrigerate for 3–4 days, turning the meat every day. Then remove the meat from the brine, rinse and cook.

Crispy-skinned baked potatoes and lightly cooked cabbage are the perfect accompaniments to delicious cold ham.

Serves 4

1 small ham
2 carrots, roughly chopped
1 stalk celery, roughly chopped
1 onion, cut in half
1 leek, roughly chopped
1 handful Brussels sprouts

For the barbecue sauce

125 ml (½ cup) orange juice
75 ml (⅓ cup) tomato ketchup
75 g (3 ounces) brown sugar
60 ml (¼ cup) Worcestershire sauce
1 ml (¼ teaspoon) cayenne pepper

To serve

4 large baking potatoes
extra virgin olive oil
salt flakes
1 green cabbage, finely shredded

COLD HAM WITH BARBECUE SAUCE

If you prefer less salty ham, place it in a pan of cold water, bring the water to a boil, discard the water, then continue as below.

Place the ham in a large pan and just cover it with cold water. Add the vegetables (the stock will be great for soup), then bring to a boil and simmer the ham for 10 minutes per 500 g (1 pound). When the time is up, turn off the heat, place a lid on the pan and set aside to cool.

Preheat your oven to 180°C (350°F), and put the potatoes in to bake – to give them a crispy skin, prick them all over, rub with extra virgin olive oil and sprinkle with salt flakes before baking.

Bring a large pan of salted water to a boil. Add the cabbage and cook for a maximum of 2 minutes then drain and shake dry.

To make the barbecue sauce, put all the ingredients in a pan over a low heat and bring to a simmer for a couple of minutes, stirring.

Remove the ham from the liquid, put it on a carving board and cut it into thick slices. Serve with the baked potatoes, cabbage and a good helping of barbecue sauce.

There is something deeply satisfying about carving a glazed ham at the table. This ham can form the centerpiece for a large family meal, and the leftover meat can be used for lunches and sandwiches for days afterwards.

Serves 10-12

2 3 kg (4 6½ pounds) ham

2 carrots, roughly chopped

1 stalk celery, roughly chopped

1 onion, cut in half

1 leek, roughly chopped

1 handful Brussels sprouts

15 ml (1 tablespoon) whole cloves

175 ml (¾ cup) orange juice

100 g (3½ ounces) brown sugar (about 250 ml/½ cup)

15 ml (1 tablespoon) mustard powder

BAKED GLAZED HAM

If you prefer less salty ham, place it in a pan of cold water, bring the water to a boil, discard the water, then continue as below.

Place the ham in a large pan and just cover it with cold water. Add the vegetables (the stock will be great for soup), bring to a boil then reduce the heat and simmer the ham for 10 minutes per 500 g (1 pound). When the time is up, turn off the heat, place a lid on the pan and set aside to cool.

Preheat the oven to 200°C (400°F). When it is cool enough to handle, take the ham out of the liquid and carefully remove the skin, leaving a layer of fat on the meat. Score the fat to produce a pattern of diamonds about 3 cm (1¼ inches) across and stick a clove into each diamond. Pour the orange juice over the ham. Then, using a fine sieve, dredge the ham first with the brown sugar and then with the mustard powder.

Bake the ham for 15 minutes then baste it with the juices (especially the ends). Return to the oven for a further 15 minutes then baste for a final time before moving it to a carving board. Allow the ham to rest for 10–15 minutes before cutting it into slices to serve.

Chaps, which come from the lower half of a pig's cheeks, are very fatty and have a distinctive, deep taste. Our favorite way of using them is as a potted meat in which the taste and texture can really be shown off and appreciated. Serve this really easy potted ham with crusty bread -- it beats conventional pâtés hands down.

Makes 2 small jars

For the chaps

2 chaps
2 carrots, roughly chopped
1 onion, cut in half
1 stalk celery

For the potted ham

2 onions, diced
zest of 1 orange
15 ml (1 tablespoon) whole-grain mustard
5 ml (1 teaspoon) Dijon mustard
1 pinch ground cloves
juice of 1 lemon
15 ml (1 tablespoon) chopped fresh thyme

To finish

75 g (3 ounces) butter (about 75 ml/⅓ cup), melted
2 sprigs fresh thyme

POTTED HAM

Place the chaps in a large pan with the carrots, onion and celery. Cover with water, bring to a boil, then reduce the heat and simmer for 3–4 hours. Remove the chaps and set aside. Boil the stock to reduce it to at least half of its original volume. When the chaps are cool enough, strip away the fat and place the meat in a large mixing bowl.

Add the potted ham ingredients to the bowl along with 30 ml (2 tablespoons) of the reduced stock and mix well. Decant the mixture into small jars, seal with a layer of melted butter and top with a sprig of thyme. Leave in the fridge to set. It will keep for 3–5 months.

Melted butter seals the dish

Rollmops are fillets of herring rolled around a collection of ingredients (usually slices of onion, pickles or green olives with pimento), and held together with a couple of wooden skewers and cured in brine. Rollmops can be eaten cold, without unrolling, or on bread. After a jar has been opened, they will usually keep for 2 to 3 weeks in the fridge.

Makes 6

1 onion, thinly sliced

1 pickle

6 filleted herrings (butterfly filleted if possible, see pages 156-157)

salt and freshly ground black pepper

500 ml (2 cups) white wine vinegar

175 ml (¾ cup) water

50 g (2 ounces) sugar (about 60 ml/¼ cup)

2 bay leaves

10 juniper berries, gently crushed

6 black peppercorns

ROLLMOPS

Bring a pan of water to a boil. Add the onion slices, blanch them for 10 seconds and then refresh in cold water. Slice the pickle lengthways into eight long slivers.

Place the herring fillets skin side down on a board. Season them with salt and pepper and lay a few slices of onion on each fillet. Place a length of pickle on top (you'll have a couple left over) and roll up the fillet, securing it with a wooden toothpick.

Place the rolled fillets into a pan that only just holds them, so they fit snugly. Add the rest of the ingredients and bring to a boil over low heat. Simmer for 1 minute, then remove from the heat and allow the fillets to cool in the liquid.

When cool, put the fillets into sterilized jars and cover with the marinade. Seal and refrigerate. They will be ready to eat after 1 week but will keep, refrigerated, for up to 6 months.

BRINED BEEF

Beef that has been cured in brine is known as salt beef, and when salt beef is cooked it is called corned beef. Beef brisket is the ideal beef cut to use – it is fatty and full of connective tissue, which makes it incredibly moist when cooked. It's very similar to pork belly, but much cheaper. Nowadays beef is becoming more and more popular for curing, with specialities like corned beef (see page 36) and pastrami (see pages 108-109) both making a comeback. The excellent thing about brining beef is that it's one of the easiest methods to do.

PREPARING THE BRINE

First make your brine. There are two different ways of adding flavorings to the brine. The first option is to put all the brine ingredients except for the salt in a large pan and bring it to a boil. Then add the salt and stir until it dissolves. Skim any scum off the surface and allow the brine to cool. Once cooled, the brine is ready to use. The aromatics can be strained out or left until the end of curing, depending on how spiced you would like the meat.

Alternatively, take all your aromatic spices and place them in a circle of cheesecloth. Gather the cheesecloth together to form a bag and secure with a little piece of string. Bash the bag with the blunt edge of a knife or a rolling pin to release the flavors. The spice bag can then be added to the cooled brine, along with the garlic cloves, or boiled in the brine prior to cooling.

CURING YOUR BRISKET

You will need a brining container with a lid or a large, heavy-duty freezer bag. The container should be the same dimensions as the piece of meat you are curing.

Pour the brine into your container and add the brisket, making sure that the meat is immersed. Put a lid on the container and refrigerate for one week, turning the meat daily.

COOKING YOUR BRISKET

After 7–10 days, remove the brisket from the brine, rinse it briefly and pat dry with papertowels. Place it in a large pan and cover with fresh water, adding a chopped carrot, an onion and celery stalk. Simmer for 3–4 hours, until you can easily run a sharp knife or skewer into the meat.

NOW TRY: SALT PORK

Salt pork is almost identical to salt beef. It can be cured with much more fat on it – cut into small, fatty lardons, it is excellent in soups or added to salami.

For 750 g (1½ pound) pork belly or pork side, dissolve 300 g (10 ounces) of salt (about 310 ml/1¼ cups) in 4 L (1 gallon) of water, add 15 ml (1 tablespoon) of pepper, 1 bay leaf, 4 whole cloves and 5 ml (1 teaspoon) each of nutmeg and mustard seeds. Submerge the pork in the brine and place in the fridge for 2–4 days. Remove the pork from the brine, rinse in cold water and pat dry before using.

A FLAVORED BRINE FOR BEEF

For 1 kg (2 pounds) beef brisket

4 L (1 gallon) water

400g (14 ounces) salt
(about 400 ml/1⅔ cups)

200 g (7 ounces) sugar
(about 250 ml/1 cup)

2 bay leaves

25 g (1 ounce) spice bag, containing equal parts allspice, juniper, mustard, coriander, dried chilies, fresh ginger and whole cloves

3 garlic cloves

Bring the water, salt, sugar and bay leaves to a boil in a pan and then allow to cool. Place the spice bag ingredients in a circle of cheesecloth, gather the edges together and tie with string.

Bash the spice bag with the blunt edge of a knife or a rolling pin to release the flavors. Peel the garlic cloves.

Pour the cooled brine into a dish and add the spice bag, garlic and beef, making sure the meat is submerged. Put a lid on the dish and place in the fridge for a week, turning daily.

This quick and easy recipe is a really unusual way to serve salt beef and makes a delicious starter, lunch or snack. The nettle mayonnaise tastes great with the salt beef. If you don't have nettles, you can use dill or watercress instead.

Serves 4

For the nettle mayonnaise

200 ml (¾ cup plus 2 tablespoons) vegetable oil, plus a little extra to cook the nettles and garlic

125 g (4 ounces) young nettle leaves

1 garlic clove, thinly sliced

1 large egg yolk

5 ml (1 teaspoon) Dijon mustard

For the beef croquettes

450 g (15½ ounces) salt beef, cooled

2 eggs

100 ml (⅓ cup plus 2 tablespoons) milk

100 ml (⅓ cup plus 2 tablespoons) beer

45 ml (3 tablespoons) mustard

5 ml (1 teaspoon) cayenne pepper

salt and freshly ground black pepper

vegetable oil, for deep-frying

SALT BEEF CROQUETTES WITH NETTLE MAYONNAISE

To make the mayonnaise, heat a little vegetable oil in a pan, then add the nettle leaves and garlic and sauté for 2 minutes. Set aside to cool.

Place the egg yolk in a blender with the mustard and blitz. When smooth, with the appliance running, pour a little of the oil into the blender until it is incorporated and the mayonnaise thickens. Stop the blender, add the cooked nettles and whiz to a puree.

Finely shred the salt beef and form it into large balls. Whisk together the eggs, milk, beer, mustard, cayenne and salt and pepper to make a batter. Dip each ball into the mixture and deep-fry at 270°C (520°F) for 2–3 minutes, or until golden brown. Drain on papertowels and serve while still warm with a lightly dressed arugala salad, the nettle mayonnaise and a few small pickles.

We think there should be a corned beef renaissance. Home-made corned beef is full of depth and flavor -- nothing like the packaged variety. This recipe takes a classic breakfast dish and turns it into a hearty dinner with some Irish charm.

Serves 4

1 kg (2 pounds) cured beef brisket

1 onion, roughly chopped

1 carrot, roughly chopped

1 stalk celery, roughly chopped

butter

2 large white onions, finely diced

4 potatoes, finely diced

30-45 ml (2-3 tablespoons) of the reduced stock from the curing process (see page 32)

15 ml (1 tablespoon) chopped parsley

IRISH CORNED BEEF HASH

To make the corned beef, put the beef brisket in a large pan and add the carrot, onion and celery. Add enough water to cover the beef, bring to a boil, then turn the heat down and simmer gently for 3 hours, turning the beef so that it is always in the liquid. Remove the beef and vegetables from the pan and set aside, and then boil the stock for 45 minutes or until it starts to thicken.

Melt a generous knob of butter in a large pan and add the onions. Cook for a few minutes then add the potatoes. Now dice the corned beef and add it to the pan along with the reduced stock. Cook for 15–20 minutes or until the potatoes and beef start to brown. Stir in the parsley and serve.

Salt pork, which is also known as white bacon, is usually made from pork belly. It has more flavor and cooks more quickly than unsalted pork. Along with the onions, potatoes and milk, salt pork is an essential component of a traditional seafood chowder.

Serves 4-6

24 clams (about 250 g/8 ounces)

25g (1 ounce) butter (about 30 ml/2 tablespoons)

150g (5oz) salt pork, finely diced

1 large leek, finely chopped

1 large onion, roughly chopped

2 stalks celery, finely chopped

500 g (1 pound) potatoes, peeled and diced

625 ml (2½ cups) milk

310 ml (1¼ cups) cream (18%)

1 bay leaf, finely chopped

salt and black and white pepper

SALT PORK & CLAM CHOWDER

Clean the clams, discarding any that are open and don't shut when you tap them, and put them into a large pan with a splash of water. Put a lid on the pan and cook over high heat for a few minutes or until all the clams have opened. Discard any that remain shut. Drain the liquid into another container and set aside – this liquid will add extra flavor to the chowder later.

When the clams have cooled enough to handle, remove most of them from their shells, setting a few aside to garnish the dish. Cut the clams into small pieces, about 1 cm (½ inch).

Melt the butter in the same pan and add the salt pork. When it starts to brown, add the leek, onion and celery and fry until soft. Put the potatoes, milk, cream and bay leaf into another large pan over medium heat and cook until the potatoes start to soften. Combine the potato mixture with the pork and onion mixture, then add the saved clam juice and simmer for 5 minutes. Finally, add the chopped clams and season with salt and white pepper.

To serve, add a few of the reserved clams in their shells to each bowl, ladle the chowder over and sprinkle with ground black pepper.

2

DRY CURING

DRY CURING

Dry curing is just the same as brining -- but without the added water. This method has been widely used as a means of preservation since ancient times. Our forebears may not have understood the chemistry, but it is relatively simple: almost all meat contains a high percentage of water, which must be removed to prevent it from spoiling. Salt rubbed into the meat draws out the water and retards the growth of enzymes and microbes.

HOW DRY CURING WORKS

If we look at our food a little more closely, we see that it has a very complex structure. When we are curing food it pays to understand the action of enzymes and micro-organisms as well as the structure of the meat. Enzymes are specialized proteins that can help foods to ripen; however, they can also trigger the rotting process. The simplest way to stop enzymes is to cook the food or to freeze it. Mold, yeast and bacteria are all microorganisms that are sometimes harnessed to add flavor (just think of ripe cheeses), but if left unchecked they may ruin your food.

The resistance of different types of bacteria to salt varies. For example, salmonella is inhibited by salt concentrations as low as 3%, but staphylococcus survives in much higher concentrations. The curing process must provide sufficient cure to effectively protect against unwanted degradation. It may sound like a battlefield, but there is the added advantage that the flavor is enhanced as well, especially if herbs or spices are added.

Good old-fashioned salt is the key ingredient, though it acts less harshly as a dry cure if used in a coarser form, so rock, kosher or sea salts are preferable to table salt. Curing does not happen instantaneously – it takes time for the salt to penetrate the meat and draw out the moisture. It is also worth remembering that the meat is vulnerable during the curing process, so it must be kept in a cool place. It was no accident that curing used to be most common at the start of winter, when the autumn reserves had diminished and the cool days had started. Using salt alone can dry out the meat and leave it hard and salty, and it often loses its color. To counteract this, sugar is usually added to the mixture.

GUIDELINES

- It is essential to buy good meat or fish.
- Clean everything that you are going to use very carefully.
- Trim the meat of excess fat and unwanted bits prior to curing.
- Rub the salt into the meat or fish thoroughly, especially into any creases or crevices.
- Use a crock or other large pot, a plastic food container or a hardwood box or barrel.
- Keep the meat or fish cool while curing.
- Curing takes time, so be patient – good things come to those who wait.

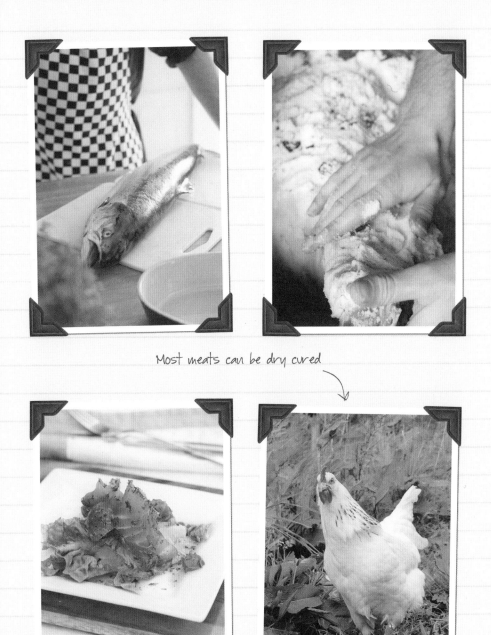

Most meats can be dry cured

It is essential to start with the best quality
meat or fish you can afford

THE ESSENTIAL CURE

To make a basic dry cure, mix salt and sugar in a ratio of 3:1 by weight. You will need at least 100 g (3½ ounce) of cure per 1 kg (2 pounds) of meat or fish. Then add your spices or flavorings. It makes sense to cure more than one cut of meat or fish at a time. For example, for 5 kg (11 pounds) of meat you would use at least 500g (1 pound) of cure – 375g (13 ounces) salt and 125g (4 ounces) sugar.

ADDING FLAVORINGS

You can customize your cure with almost any flavoring, but lightly ground spices will impart more flavor than herbs, especially if the spices have been lightly toasted before grinding to release their oils. Use aromatic spices like dried chilies, star anise, black peppercorns and cardamom pods. Instead of sugar you can add honey or even molasses.

THE CURING PROCESS

You will need a plastic tub, a crock or other large pot or a hardwood box or barrel. The container must have drainage holes and must not be made of metal. Rub the individual joints of meat or pieces of fish thoroughly with the cure, taking care to include any crevices and areas around the bones. Spread a good layer of cure at the bottom of the container, and then add the largest pieces of meat or fish, skin side down, trying not to let them touch. Cover with a layer of cure then add a second layer of meat or fish. Cover with more cure. Put a lid on the container, preferably weighing it down on the meat. Place the container on a drainer or tray, and store in a cool place for 4 days, making sure the liquid that comes out of the bottom of your container can drain away.

After 4 days remove the meat from the container and repack it all, making sure that it is well covered with the cure. If some areas appear to have been left bare, rub the cure into them thoroughly. The meat should now remain in this second cure for 2 days per 1 kg (2 pounds). Make sure you put the smaller pieces on top, because they do not need to cure for as long as the larger ones and you'll want to take them out first.

TIMING CONSIDERATIONS

There are lots of variables when you are determining the length of curing:
- In cold weather, the curing can take longer, and if it is warm the curing time is shorter.
- Thick cuts need more curing time than thin ones.
- Personal taste is a factor.

DRY CURES AND TIMING

PRODUCT	SALT	SUGAR	TIME
DUCK, BREASTS about 1 kg (2 pounds)	100 g (3½ ounces) (about 125 ml/½ cup)	30g (1¼ ounces) (about 37 ml/ 2½ tablespoons)	6 days
PORK, BELLY OR BACK about 2 kg (4 pounds)	2 kg (4 pounds) (about 2 L/8 cups)	200g (7 ounces) (about 250 ml/1 cup)	8 days
LEG OF PORK about 6 kg (13 pounds)	600g (1¼ pound) (about 625 ml/ 2½ cups)	200g (7 ounces) (about 250 ml/1 cup)	21 days

DRY-CURED PORK

Dry curing different cuts of pork will produce a variety of completely different tastes and textures. We particularly enjoy chaps, hocks and collar of bacon, but apart from the fillet, which is an expensive and very tender cut, there is no part of the pig that doesn't warrant a cure. Dry curing a whole leg results in something impressive, but, that said, everyone should really start with bacon.

CHOOSING YOUR CUT

If you are inexperienced or lack confidence in your butchery skills, ask your butcher to prepare the meat for you. Although it is quite long, a whole piece of pork that has the loin meat and the belly meat is a bit special and is very easy to cold-smoke after it has been cured (see page 142). Ask your butcher for collar if you want a meaty, well-marbled bacon.

PREPARING THE CURE

Mix together the cure ingredients. For a boned back and belly of pork weighing about 2 kg (4 pounds), you'll need 200 g (7 ounces) of

rock salt (about 250 ml/1 cup) and 75g (3 ounces) of brown sugar. For your first foray into making bacon it is best to use just salt and sugar; however, if you are adding any spices or herbs, do it at this stage, after crushing them with a pestle and mortar.

Curing a whole leg may seem like a large undertaking, but the principles remain the same whatever the size of the piece of meat – just use the same proportions of salt and sugar.

COMPLETING THE CURE

After 4 days, take the pork out of the container and brush any remaining cure back into the container. The meat will have changed texture, becoming firmer. Rub the cure into the pork again and pack it back into the box. If any areas are smooth and appear not to have been cured, rub extra cure into them and make sure that they are in contact with lots of salt mixture. After another 2 days, repeat the process. Do this once more, making the total cure time 8 days. Finally, rinse with cold water, pat dry with papertowels and then hang in a cool place to dry thoroughly before you pack and refrigerate it.

Remember that personal taste is paramount. Always make notes about what you've done and adjust accordingly to make sure that you achieve your desired cure next time.

Start with bacon

HOW TO DRY-CURE PORK

AN AROMATIC CURE FOR A LEG OF PORK

For a 6 kg (13-pound) leg of pork

600 g (1¼ pounds) salt (about 625 ml/2½ cups)

200 g (7 ounce) sugar

10 whole star anise

10 bay leaves

45 ml (3 tablespoons) black peppercorns

45 ml (3 tablespoons) coriander seeds

6 dried chilies

Lightly crush the spices with a pestle and mortar and put them in a bowl with the salt and sugar.

Rub some of the cure into your meat. Place a layer of the curing mix in a plastic or hardwood container. The container should have drainage holes in the bottom and a lid.

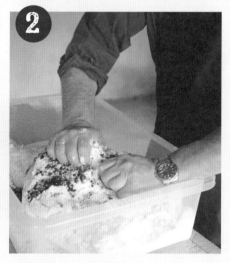

Lay the meat on the cure, fat side down. Sprinkle on another layer of cure, and if you have more meat, repeat the process.

If there is any cure left over at the end, pack it all around the pork. Cover with a clean kitchen cloth and store in a cool place to allow to cure.

This recipe makes a rich sauce that clings to the pasta, but the crispy, salty bacon flavor is the star. Home-made pesto is best, but you can buy it ready-made if you prefer.

Serves 4

500 g (1 pound) dried pasta (linguine is best for this)

5 ml (1 teaspoon) olive oil

200 g (7 ounces) dry-cured bacon, cut into small pieces

½ onion, finely diced

10 sun-dried tomatoes, finely chopped

175 ml (¾ cup) crème fraîche or sour cream

For the pesto

1 handful fresh basil leaves

3 garlic cloves

15 ml (1 tablespoon) pine nuts

15 ml (1 tablespoon) grated Parmesan cheese

extra virgin olive oil

PASTA WITH BACON & PESTO

To make the pesto, use a mortar and pestle, a blender or a food processor to bash or blend the basil, garlic, pine nuts, Parmesan and sufficient extra virgin olive oil to make a thick paste. Set aside.

Bring a large pan of salted water to a boil. Add the pasta and the teaspoon of oil to the water and cook so it is still quite firm, being careful not to overcook it.

While the pasta is cooking, put the bacon in a large frying pan without any oil and cook over high heat until it starts to crisp. Add the onions and cook for another 3 minutes, then stir in the pesto and the sun-dried tomatoes and cook for a further 3 minutes. Stir in the crème fraîche or sour cream. Set aside.

Drain the pasta when it's ready. Add it to the pan of sauce, stir to coat and serve.

Nothing beats fresh pesto

METHOD #4

DRY-CURED DUCK BREASTS

Duck breast is a relatively expensive meat, but its richness means it can go quite a long way. If it's served conventionally, either pan-fried or roasted, people tend to expect a whole breast, but if it's cured then sliced and cooked, a single breast can easily serve three people. There is the added advantage that the curing process preserves the meat, so it can be kept in the fridge and makes an easy, quick and very tasty meal.

PREPARING THE CURE

The process couldn't be simpler. Mix your cure ingredients together. Then place a layer of cure in a container with drainage holes. Rub some cure into the breasts, place them skin side down on top of the cure in the container and sprinkle a layer of cure on top.

COMPLETING THE CURE

After 4 days, take the duck breasts out of the curing box and brush any remaining cure back into the box. The breasts will have changed texture, becoming firmer. Rub the cure into the flesh again and pack the breasts back into the box. If any areas are smooth and appear not to have been cured, rub extra cure into them and make sure that they are in contact with lots of cure. Depending on their thickness, they will need 1 or 2 days more – the finished cured breast should not give easily when pressed between your thumb and finger. When the duck breasts are cured, rinse off any remaining salt with cold water and dry with papertowels. Hang up the breasts and allow to dry thoroughly. Store in the fridge for 2–3 weeks.

NOW TRY: TURKEY

Curing turkey meat can also be very successful, but it has to be the dark meat – the breast and other white meat is too lean for curing and treating like ham. However, if you lightly cure the meat it can be hot-smoked (see pages 112–113) and is truly delicious.

AN AROMATIC CURE FOR DUCK BREASTS

For 4 duck breasts, weighing about 1 kg (2 pounds)

1 orange

3 whole star anise

1 dried chili

100 g (3½ ounces) rock salt

30g (1¼ ounces) brown sugar

1 small bunch fresh thyme

Use a vegetable peeler to remove the zest from the orange. Crush the spices with a pestle and mortar and put them in a bowl with the salt and sugar.

HOW TO DRY-CURE DUCK BREASTS

Trim any loose fat or blood off the breasts and then prick each breast with a skewer on the skin side, piercing about halfway through and making about 12 holes in each breast.

Place a layer of the cure in a container with drainage holes in the bottom. Then rub some of the cure mixture into each duck breast.

Put a layer of duck breasts on top of the cure, skin side down. Sprinkle on another layer of cure, then add another layer of breasts, skin side down, and top with the rest of the cure.

Cover and store in a cool place for 4 days. Then remove the breasts from the container, rub cure into the meat again, repack in the container and cure for 1–2 more days.

When cooked, dry-cured duck breast has the characteristics of lean bacon, but it keeps its own unique flavor. Deep-frying the duck for just a few moments produces crispy slices that are delicious scattered over a salad. The salty duck and sweet oranges in this recipe are beautifully complemented by bitter salad leaves.

Serves 4

vegetable oil, for deep-frying

1 dry-cured duck breast, thinly sliced

2 blood oranges

50 g (2 ounces) butter
(about 45 ml (3 tablespoons)

50 g (2 ounces) brown sugar (about 60 mL/¼ cup)

2–3 handfuls of mixed salad leaves

For the dressing

60 ml (¼ cup) extra virgin olive oil

30 ml (2 tablespoons) cider vinegar

15 ml (1 tablespoon) finely grated orange zest

2 ml (½ teaspoon) mustard

CRISPY DRY-CURED DUCK SALAD WITH CARAMELIZED ORANGES

To make the salad dressing, mix together the ingredients in a small bowl or jug.

Heat some oil in a deep-fryer or a large pan and deep-fry the slices of duck for a few moments. If you don't have a deep fryer, heat a little oil in a frying pan and cook the slices one layer at a time.

Cut the peel and pith off the oranges, and then cut the fruit horizontally into slices about 5 mm (¼ inch) thick. Heat the butter and sugar in a hot frying pan until the mixture bubbles. Dab the orange slices with papertowel and add them to the pan. Do not move them around; let them cook in one position. After 4 minutes the orange slices should be caramelized, so turn them over and cook the other side.

Take the pan off the heat and set the oranges aside to cool. Add the pan juices to the dressing.

Arrange the salad leaves in a serving dish and scatter the duck and orange slices over the top. Drizzle with the dressing and serve.

METHOD #5

GRAVLAX

This method of dry curing was developed in
Scandinavia as a way of preserving the seasonal
glut of salmon. Fresh fish were buried in the sand
with salt and herbs and retrieved days, weeks
or months later after they had "fermented" and
become palatable. Today fermentation is no longer
a part of the process, but salmon is still "buried"
in a dry marinade. The same method can be used
to cure any oily, firm-fleshed fish, including trout.
It's a great way to make a side of salmon last for many meals -- once cured it
will keep for about a week in the refrigerator. Once you've mastered gravlax,
experiment with flavors and try them with your favorite fish.

HOW TO FILLET YOUR FISH

Preparing your own fresh-caught fish is the ultimate experience, and starting with a whole one
is the most cost-effective option if you're buying one. You can ask your fish dealer to do it for
you, but filleting a whole fish is a skill worth having – and it's easy when you know how.

Gut and clean your fish if you need to and pat
it dry. Make an incision with a sharp filleting
knife just behind the gills on one side, from
the top of the head to the belly.

Now begin to slice from the top of the
fish down the backbone, all the way from
head to tail, separating the flesh from the
bone as you go.

Pulling up the flesh as you work, scrape along the backbone in the direction of the tail to loosen the fillet.

Slice all the way through the skin on the belly as you work your way to the tail. Once you've removed the first fillet, set it aside, flip the fish over and repeat on the other side.

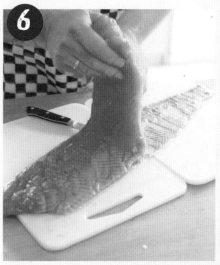

Before you skin a fillet, remove any bones that remain in the flesh. Be especially wary of pin bones, which are very unpleasant if swallowed. Feel for bones with your fingers, and remove them with a pair of tweezers.

Finally, skin your fillet. Starting at the tail, use the knife blade to wiggle along the skin and separate the flesh in one piece. Trim your fillet if needed. Use the leftover skin, head and bones to make fish stock.

A CLASSIC SALMON GRAVLAX

For a 750 g (1½ pound) side of salmon

1 large bunch fresh dill, chopped

100 g (3½ ounces) sugar
(about 125ml/ ½ cup)

sea salt

black pepper

Mix the dill and sugar in a bowl, and season with a large pinch of salt and a few grinds of pepper to taste. Then follow the step by step instructions on this page.

Put half the dill mixture in the bottom of a glazed, flat-bottomed baking dish and set the salmon on top.

Coat the salmon evenly with the remaining dill mixture.

Cover with a loose sheet of plastic wrap and put a press on top (see next page). Weight the top – evenly placed cans from your pantry are ideal – and refrigerate for 24 hours.

MAKE YOUR OWN PRESS

Any glazed container can be used as a press -- it doesn't matter what shape the dish is as long as it is large enough to contain a side of fish. Using your container as a guide, cut a piece of wood that sits snugly inside the dish on the bottom. To help make it easy to remove the lid from the dish, add a wooden handle to the top of the lid with a stainless steel screw.

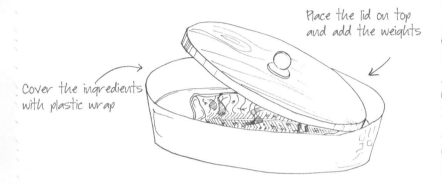

Place the lid on top and add the weights

Cover the ingredients with plastic wrap

PREPARING THE CURE

The dill cure of classic gravlax is hard to beat, but other flavors work well too. Try replacing the dill and black pepper with the zest of both a lemon and orange or 45 ml (3 tablespoons) of grated horseradish.

FINISHING IT OFF

Before serving, rinse the gravlax thoroughly under cold water to remove all trace of the curing mixture. Blot with papertowels to dry. Cover one side of the fillet completely with finely chopped dill tops, avoiding the stems, which are bitter. Cover completely with foil and refrigerate until needed.

SERVING IT UP

Place the gravlax, dill side up, on a flat surface. Using a filleting knife, slice diagonally across the breadth of the fillet to give thin, even slices. Each slice should have a strip of dill along one edge.

SALT COD

There are a few dishes that really epitomize the curing process, and salt cod is one of them. It oozes history and sums up traditional preserving techniques. It's also incredibly practical and easy to try at home with only two ingredients: salt and cod. The process evolved as a method of preserving fish in hot countries, where it was first salted and then dried in the sun. But salting cod will work anywhere, as long as you have a dry place to store it. We love the taste, but be aware that the cod will not look particularly attractive when it has been rehydrated and is therefore best used as an ingredient in other dishes.

HOW TO SALT A FILLET OF COD

The large white flakes of cod make it perfect for salting. It is possible to salt a fish like haddock, but other white fish tend to be too fine flaked, so when reconstituted can become mushy. For one fresh fillet of cod you will need 400 g (14 ounces) of salt (about 500 ml/2 cups).

First, wash and dry the fish. Then find a large tray and cover it with salt. Place the cod fillet on the salt and sprinkle more salt over the top, until covered.

Use your hands to gently massage the salt into the crevices and evenly cover the cod in a generous layer of salt.

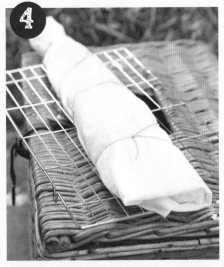

Pack the salt onto the fish and transfer it to a sheet of muslin or cheesecloth. Wrap the fish in a double layer of the fabric, using string to hold it gently in place.

Place the freshly wrapped fish on a wire rack with a tray beneath it. Place it in the fridge and leave for 24 hours.

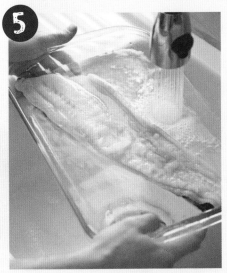

REHYDRATING SALT COD

After 24 hours, unwrap the fish and rinse well in cold water. Rewrap with a single layer of muslin or cheesecloth and place in a dish. Leave for 1 week, turning the fish and discarding any liquid daily. Store for up to 9 months in the fridge.

To rehydrate the cod, soak it for 24 hours in cold water, changing the water a few times to remove some of the saltiness.

Fish pie takes many different guises, and this recipe is our twist on a salt cod version. The mornay sauce gives it a rich, creamy texture and a golden brown topping. We like to serve this with boiled new potatoes, mixed with capers and lemon zest, and a parsnip puree.

Serves 4

For the cod

800 g (1 ¾ pound) salt cod, desalted

1 bouquet garni containing sprigs of fresh thyme, parsley and bay leaves (to be used when you desalt the cod, optional)

500 g (1 pound) spinach

50 g (2 ounces) butter, plus more for the gratin dish

75 g (3 ounces) Parmesan cheese, grated

chopped fresh parsley and chives

For the mornay sauce

40 g (1½ ounces) butter (about 37 ml / 2½ tablespoons)

20 g (¾ ounce) flour (about 37 ml/2½ tablespoons)

425 ml (1¾ cups) milk

75 g (3 ounces) Gruyère cheese, grated

2 egg yolks, beaten

30 ml (2 tablespoons) 40% cream

salt and freshly ground black pepper

SALT COD FISH PIE

To make the sauce, melt the butter and stir in the flour a little at a time until the mixture resembles a smooth, shiny paste. Next add the milk a little at a time, using a whisk to mix it in. Completely incorporate each addition of milk before adding the next one. You should end up with a glossy sauce. Add the Gruyère cheese and stir until it melts. Remove the sauce from the heat and add the egg yolks. Return to the heat and bring to a boil for a final time and then take off the heat. Stir the cream into the sauce and season with salt and pepper.

Preheat the oven to 200°C (400°F).

Put the salt cod in a pan, cover it with water and add the bouquet garni. Bring to a boil, reduce to a simmer and poach for 5–6 minutes, until the fish has lost its opaque appearance and the flesh is white. Drain then flake the fish using a fork, taking care to remove any bones.

Bring a large pan of water to a boil. Add the spinach, blanch for 5 minutes, and then drain, squeezing all the water out of the leaves. Melt the butter in a large pan, add the spinach and cook over low heat for 5–10 minutes. Line a buttered gratin dish with the spinach, put the cod on top, and pour the mornay sauce over. Sprinkle with the Parmesan and bake until brown and bubbling.

Sprinkle with the parsley and chives and serve.

SALTED CAPERS

Capers are the flower buds of the caper bush (*Capparis spinosa*), a plant that grows particularly well in arid conditions, for example in Sicily, where capers are used in dishes such as puttanesca sauce. We use capers in a range of dishes, from salads to pizzas and even in our fish cakes. If you can't find fresh caper buds, you can use the same technique with nasturtium seeds before they are ripe, and we've also enjoyed experimenting with chive buds, wild garlic and elderberries. The piquancy is drawn out by the simple curing process, and, once salted, the capers will keep for about a year. You can use them as a really interesting addition to salads, fish or pasta sauce.

PICKING THE BUDS & SEEDS

If you're lucky enough to have a caper bush, pick the unopened flower buds before they ripen. Otherwise, you can use any of the following: chive buds, wild garlic, nasturtium seeds and even elderberries.

If you want to use chives or wild garlic instead of capers, pick the buds before they flower. Nasturtium seeds are best picked just after the flowers have shed their petals and while they are still firm and green – they are close in size to a traditional caper. Pick elderberries when the fruit is not quite ripe and remember to leave enough on the tree for the birds.

SALTING YOUR CAPERS

To transform the buds and seeds into capers, put them into a jam jar and completely cover them with rock salt. Leave for 4–6 hours, then wipe off as much of the salt as you can and store them in a clean, airtight jar with a few peppercorns. Don't worry too much about getting off all the salt, as the oils that have been drawn out can leave a small salty residue that is helpful for the preserving process. You may like to soak the capers for 10–15 minutes before use, though, to reduce the saltiness.

NOW TRY: HERBS

Following the same method as for the capers, you can also cure herbs for storage. Choose herbs that are at their best and harvest them

OUR SALTED MIXED HERB SEASONING

This seasoning can be stored in the fridge and is very convenient to add straight into soups, sauces, stews or even omelets.

45 ml (3 tablespoons) grated carrot
45 ml (3 tablespoons) chopped spring onions
a selection of chopped green herbs, such as chives, parsley, chervil, marjoram and savory
coarse salt

Mix together the carrot, spring onions and chopped herbs. Put the mixture in the bottom of a glass bowl and sprinkle it with thick layer of coarse salt. Cover the bowl and then place it in the fridge for a couple of weeks. Drain off the liquid that is drawn out of the herbs and vegetables, then put the salted mix in a sterilized jar and store in the fridge.

in easy-to-handle sprigs. Pack the herbs into an airtight container, such as a jam jar, and pack coarse salt round them. The herbs will keep fresh for a couple of months if stored in a dark, dry cupboard. These salted herbs are perfect for slow-cooked roasts in the months when the herbs outside are struggling because the weather has turned cold.

Salted sprigs of herbs

Preserved lemons are widely used in North African cooking, particularly in Moroccan cuisine. Adding them to rice or couscous dishes instead of salt will give your food an amazing lemon scent.

Makes 1 large jar

5 ml (1 teaspoon) coriander seeds

5 ml (1 teaspoon) black peppercorns

5 ml (1 teaspoon) fennel seeds

½ stick cinnamon, roughly crushed

150 g (5 ounce) rock or sea salt, not table salt

3 bay leaves, crushed

9 unwaxed lemons

30 ml (2 tablespoons) white wine vinegar

LEMON & HERBS IN SALT

Put the whole spices and cinnamon in a small frying pan and heat for a minute to release the flavors. Put them into a bowl with the salt and crushed bay leaves and mix together.

Make 4–5 vertical cuts into the lemons, through the peel and about halfway through the flesh. Push the spiced salt into the cuts in the lemons, and then squeeze them into a large, airtight jar. Shake the last of the spiced salt over the lemons to coat them when they are in situ.

Push the lemons firmly down into the jar, and then pour in the white wine vinegar and enough cold water to just cover them. Put the lid on the jar and store in a cool place.

These lemons will be ready to eat after about a month and will keep unopened for a couple of years. Each time you remove one, make sure the liquid still covers the lemons and that you reseal the jar.

3

AIR DRYING

AIR DRYING

Air drying is one of the oldest methods of preserving and drying food, and it is just a step up from brining or dry curing. In hot climates food can be dried in the sunshine to increase its storage time. In cooler regions air drying is a slower process but can still be achieved with good ventilation. A degree of humidity in the air isn't a bad thing - don't worry about some moisture because it will prevent your salami from going too wrinkly. If you live near the coast, a slight sea breeze is actually a good thing. The keys to effective drying are good air circulation, a fairly constant temperature and avoiding direct contact with moisture.

HOW AIR DRYING WORKS

Air drying is pretty much as simple as it sounds. Drying meat and fish requires more work than fruit and vegetables, but the approach is similar for all of them. The basic technique is to hang cured meat outside so that air can pass over it and draw out any moisture, thus preventing the growth of unwanted bacteria and fungi.

GUIDELINES

- Cure your meat or fish before air drying.
- Separate items that are drying to maximize air flow.
- Check on your meat or fish every couple of weeks and keep an eye out for mold.
- Clean your air-dried product thoroughly with a stiff brush and vinegar before eating.
- Trust your nose – if something smells wrong, don't risk eating it.

THE CURING PROCESS

Before preparing to air-dry something it is important to give it a head start, especially in temperate regions where there is plenty of rain in the air and not much sun. In these circumstances meat and fish should always be cured before you even think about air drying. The curing process can be done by brining (pages 18–21) or by dry salt cure (pages 42–45). Generally, you want to be able to hang up the cut of meat knowing that it has already had a lot of moisture sucked out of it. Smaller cuts such as bacon will obviously need less time than a large leg of ham, but both need salt to aid the process. Once the salt cure has done its work, scrub off any remaining salt or wash off the brine solution and pat the meat or fish dry.

THE PERFECT WRAP

What you wrap your chosen item in is almost as important as where you air-dry it. Muslin and cheesecloth are ideal, as they're cheap, easy to find and allow a really good flow of air. Try to wrap the meat or fish in just a single layer otherwise you will not allow enough air in to help with evaporation. Another material that works very well is fine cloth netting, available online and from specialty kitchen stores. Use string to secure the wrapping around the meat or fish and butcher's hooks to hang it up.

From magnificent air-dried legs of ham to spicy salamis, flavoring is key

A couple of hours of effort = a handful of chorizo

A DRYING BOX

If you don't have a covered outbuilding or
shed, you can make yourself a drying box. All
you need is some screening or fine material
for the sides and bottom of the box, a wooden
roof or a metal garbage can lid to deflect the
rain, and a strong hook to hang the box from
the eaves of your house or from a tree branch.
Try to make it large enough so that no part of
the product is in direct contact with the sides
or bottom of the box. You really want the
product to be suspended inside. Alternatively,
you could try adapting an old cheese safe or
making a wire mesh cage. The most important
aspect is to make sure that air can fly through
but insects and animals can't get in.

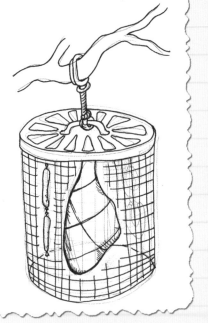

HANGING LOCATIONS

The key to successful air drying is to place your wrapped investment somewhere where it can hang for a long time – anything from 2 to 24 months. It needs to be:

- High enough to be out of reach of animals and children.
- Not in your way – you don't want to bang your head on it.
- Under cover, avoiding rainfall.
- In an open place with good all-round air circulation.
- Ideally somewhere where there's a through draft.
- Not in direct sunlight.
- Not in complete darkness.
- If possible, in an area that can maintain a fairly constant temperature.

THE MECHANICAL ALTERNATIVE

A more controlled way to air-dry indoors is to buy an electric dehydrator or food dryer. Both appliances will speed up the natural process of moisture being drawn out the food. The fact that they are controllable means you can predict when your food is done, which is a significant advantage compared to letting the natural flow of air do the drying.

These specialty gadgets create the perfect environment for drying. With internal ventilation and the ability to adjust the temperature, they are great for meat and vegetables. The downside is that they don't come cheap. One way to improvise your own would be to take an old cupboard, install some wire shelving inside and then place an electric fan at the bottom. Then, cut a few holes at the top, the same size as wine corks, and control the air-flow by adding or removing corks to restrict or increase it.

HOW LONG DOES IT TAKE?

The longer you air-dry your product, the longer it will keep and the more the flavors will intensify.

PRODUCT	DRYING TIME
Air-dried ham	4–18 months
Mojama (tuna loin)	1 month
Bresaola (beef)	3 weeks
Jerky	2 weeks
Mutton	1 month
Salami	1–2 months

Enjoy with flakes of Parmesan

METHOD #8

AIR-DRIED HAM

Genuine Parma ham is one of Italy's most famous foods -- the ultimate air-dried ham. Every year we make our own version using this simple method. Follow the instructions closely and use the precise ingredients specified in order to avoid spoiling your meat. Any cut of meat will do, and a whole leg is a showstopper, but we like to cure a boned leg for everyday eating. You could also consider starting with something smaller, like a piece of bacon or the chaps. This will give you the chance to alter the flavors in your cure until you have created your own secret spice combination and are ready for a large air-dried ham.

PREPARING THE CURE

Buy more salt than you think you'll require, as you will have to add extra during the process to replace the briny by-product that is drawn out of the ham. We use plain table salt because it's inexpensive and works quickly. Pour your flavored cure into a large plastic container, ideally one with a lid and with holes drilled in the bottom so that the liquid brine can drip away from the meat.

CURING YOUR HAM

Put the meat in the container and rub the cure evenly into it with your hands. Work it in all over the pork skin, making sure you include all the little flaps and crevices. Then cover the pork completely with the cure. Place the container on a large plastic tray and leave it somewhere cool for at least 10 days – in your fridge if there is room. Check the container every couple of days and pour away any brine that has formed. Brine may occur when the water is drawn out of the meat and

mixes with the salt. When this happens, add more salt and rub the cure back into the meat.

PREPARING TO DRY

After 16 days in the cure, remove the meat and brush off all of the cure mixture, using a stiff brush and a generous amount of apple cider vinegar. Wrap the ham in a large, clean piece of muslin or cheesecloth and tie it up securely with string.

HANGING YOUR HAM

Now hang the meat outside in a dry but well-ventilated area. Butcher's hooks are worth investing in for this. Leave the ham hanging in a shed or under an overhang for at least 18 weeks. The longer you leave it, the more intense the flavor and the dryer the meat. Remember that when you eventually take down the ham and start eating it, the process is over and you can't just hang it up again.

FINISHING IT OFF

After at least 18 weeks hanging, remove the muslin or cheesecloth and scrub off any surface mold with apple cider vinegar. Then trim off any yellow fat and some of the excess white fat. Pat dry with papertowels or a clean tea towel.

SERVING IT UP

Use a sharp knife to carve the ham into thin strips. Always keep the piece from the first cut as a type of seal. Slice from the hoof to the shortest part of the ham. Rub fat on this piece and recover the exposed meat after each time you carve. Cover it with a tea towel and keep it at room temperature. You can buy specialty wooden stands for the ham to be carved on.

NOW TRY: MOJAMA

Mojama is a chunky tuna fillet that has been air dried – traditionally for at least a month – and is from the hot and windy coast of Spain. The drying reduces the weight by half, and the result is an intense-tasting treat that keeps for several weeks in the fridge. To make mojama, cure a section of tuna loin in the salt/sugar mix for 2 days then air-dry for 3–4 weeks.

A FLAVORED CURE FOR AIR-DRIED HAM

For each 6 kg (13 pound) leg of pork

3 dried chilies

5 garlic cloves

1 large handful fresh thyme

4 whole star anise

15 ml (1 tablespoon) coriander seeds

15 ml (1 tablespoon) cumin seeds

12 whole cloves

1 handful black peppercorns

3 kg (6½ pounds) salt (about 3 L/12 cups)

1 kg (2 pounds) sugar (about 1.25 L/5 cups)

Crumble the red chilies into a mortar with the garlic, herbs and spices, grind them with a pestle to a coarse powder and then mix this well into the salt and sugar.

NOW TRY: BRESAOLA

This is made from a single beef muscle. Prepare the beef by trimming off any fat and sinews, leaving the silverskin that runs down the center of the joint. Make a simple dry cure from 100 g (3½ ounces) each of salt and sugar (about 125 ml/½ cup of each). Add herbs and spices as required (rosemary with lots of black peppercorns works very well), and seal in a freezer bag. Turn daily and leave in the fridge for a week. After a week, clean the beef and repeat the curing process. Reseal and leave for another week. Use papertowels to rub off the cure, and hang up the meat, wrapped in muslin or cheescloth. After 3 weeks it should have lost about a third of its original weight and be ready to slice thinly and enjoy with olive oil.

The air-dried ham provides the saltiness needed to bring out the flavors of the fish. The slices of monkfish wrapped in ham look spectacular, so give it a try; you won't be disappointed.

Serves 4

2 fillets of monkfish, about 150 g (5 ounces) each and 5 cm (2 inches) in diameter

4 large slices of air-dried ham

8 fresh sage leaves

salt and freshly ground black pepper

250 g (8 ounces) young green beans, topped and tailed

15 ml (1 tablespoon) extra virgin olive oil

30 ml (2 tablespoons) diced tomatoes

15 ml (1 tablespoon) lemon juice

zest of 1 lemon

ROAST MONKFISH & SAGE IN AIR-DRIED HAM

Preheat the oven to 180°C (350°F). Trim the monkfish of any colored flesh.

Lay two slices of air-dried ham side by side on your work surface and put four sage leaves in a row down the middle (pulling off the stalks if they are woody). Place a monkfish fillet on top and season with a little black pepper. Fold one edge of the ham over the fish and tuck it in, and then neatly roll the other edge of ham over and fix it in place with a couple of toothpicks or skewers.

Place the fish in a roasting pan with the sage leaves uppermost, then repeat with the second fillet. Put the roasting pan into the oven and bake for 8 minutes. When ready, the fish should feel firm to the touch.

Meanwhile, bring a large pan of salted water to a boil and blanch the beans for a minute or so. Drain then return them to the pan and toss them with the olive oil and tomatoes. Add the lemon juice and season with salt and pepper. Don't overcook the beans, as you want their texture to complement the firmness of the fish.

Remove the fish from the oven and allow to rest for at least 3 minutes in a warm place. Slice and serve with the beans, garnished with a little lemon zest.

In Spain it's a common sight to see ham croquettes served as a tapa, a light snack that's enjoyed when having a drink. This recipe allows a little of your valuable air-dried ham to go a long way. We like to eat these croquettes with salsa verde and a mixed salad.

Serves 4

For the filling

75 g (3 ounces) butter (about 75 ml/⅓ cup)

45 ml (3 heaping tablespoons) flour

175 ml (¾ cup) milk

75 g (3 ounces) cheese, grated

2 ml (½ teaspoon) Dijon mustard

5 ml (1 teaspoon) Worcestershire sauce

30 ml (2 tablespoons) finely chopped air-dried ham

vegetable oil, for deep-frying

For the coating

30 ml (2 tablespoons) flour

1 egg, beaten

50 g (2 ounces) bread crumbs (about 75 ml/⅓ cup)

50 g (2 ounces) rolled oats (about 150 ml/⅔ cup)

HAM & CHEESE CROQUETTES

To make the filling, melt the butter in a pan over low heat and add the flour, stirring continuously. Cook and stir for about 2 minutes, then remove from the heat and add the milk, a little at a time, stirring continuously to prevent lumps from forming. Return the pan to the heat and cook for about 10 minutes, to make sure the flour is cooked properly.

Add the cheese, mustard and Worcestershire sauce and stir until the cheese has melted. Remove from the heat and stir in the chopped ham until evenly distributed. Transfer the mixture to a bowl, lay a piece of plastic wrap across the surface and allow to cool before transferring to the fridge to chill.

When the mixture is thoroughly chilled and firm you can make your croquettes. First, for the coating, arrange three shallow bowls in a row and put the flour in the first, the beaten egg in the second and the bread crumbs and oatmeal, mixed together, in the third.

Form the cheese and ham mixture into eight oval-shaped croquettes. Roll them in the flour until well covered, tapping off the excess. Next, dip them in egg until well covered, letting the excess drip off. Finally, roll the croquettes in bread crumbs and set them aside on a plate.

Heat the oil to 180°C (350°F) in a deep fryer or a large pan. Add the croquettes a few at a time, so as not to lower the temperature of the oil, and cook until golden brown.

Serve the croquettes with a mixed salad.

This cured and air-dried tuna is delicious with olives and a small glass of beer. The oils in the toasted almonds really bring out the flavor, and we can't think of another food that works as well with the rich flavors of the tuna loin.

Serves 4

100 g (3½ ounces) mojama
extra virgin olive oil
40 g (1½ ounces) whole almonds
sea salt

MOJAMA WITH ALMONDS

Slice the dried tuna very thinly, so that it is almost transparent, and place it on a plate that has a raised lip. Drench in olive oil – enough to completely cover the tuna – and leave to marinate for at least 1 hour.

Meanwhile, toast the whole almonds in a dry pan until you start to smell them.

Arrange the mojama on a platter, sprinkled with the toasted almonds and sea salt. Serve with olives and crusty bread.

A little goes a long way

AIR-DRIED MUTTON

Charcuterie is generally thought of as a Mediterranean speciality that goes hand in hand with ancient olive groves and abundant vineyards. But in cooler climates there is a rich tradition of curing and smoking at home that has come from years of experience. A polar opposite to the image conjured up by a classic such as Parma ham is air-dried mutton. It is a speciality famous in areas of Scotland, where legs of mutton were brined and then dried above the smoky peat fires of many a rural croft. Now it's once again growing in popularity, and if you haven't tried it yet, it's a must. Once you've made it, try replacing the air-dried ham in any recipe with air-dried mutton instead -- the flavor is subtly different but still delicious.

CURING YOUR MUTTON

Place the mutton in a large plastic container and add the flavored brine. Put the lid on the container and leave for a week, making sure the mutton stays completely submerged – a

A FLAVORED BRINE FOR AIR-DRIED MUTTON

For a 2.5 kg (5½ pound) leg of mutton

2 kg (4 pounds) salt (about 2L/8 cups)

8 liters (2 gallons) water

2 bay leaves

1 whole star anise

5 ml (1 teaspoon) chopped fresh ginger

15 ml (1 tablespoon) pink peppercorns

15 ml (1 tablespoon) coriander seeds

Make up a brine solution with normal table salt and water until dissolved (see page 18 for more details). You'll know it's salty enough when a potato floats in it! Add the herbs and spices.

ceramic flowerpot works surprisingly well to prevent it from floating. After the mutton has spent 7 days in the curing solution, pour off the liquid, replace with fresh brine and leave for a further 2 weeks.

DRYING & FINISHING

Remove the mutton from the brine. Pat the mutton dry with papertowels, then wrap in muslin or cheesecloth and tie with string (see below). Hang it up in a sheltered but well-ventilated area for a further 8–16 weeks. Then remove the wrappings and clean the mutton with apple cider vinegar and a stiff brush before carving.

SERVING IT UP

Air drying concentrates flavors and firms up the flesh. When you cut the meat very thinly across the grain it does not matter how tough the meat was before curing and drying: it will now be easy to chew.

Compared to a normal portion of meat for a meal, air-dried meat should be eaten sparingly because of the high salt level and the richness. of the flavor. Serve a little air-dried mutton as an antipasto or try eating it with bread and a sweet chutney for a delicious snack.

NOW TRY: GOAT

If you want a change, why not try air-drying goat? Goat meat is nice and lean, so it's perfectly suited to curing and especially to air drying. Follow the same method as for the mutton, or try air-drying it as thin strips of jerky (see pages 94–5) for a week first.

HOW TO WRAP A LEG OF MUTTON

When wrapping the leg of mutton in muslin or cheesecloth, cover the leg completely in a single layer of material. This will provide protection from insects but won't restrict air flow.

Tie the wrappings firmly in place with string. It is important to make sure the string will not move during the months of drying.

When we heard about the process of air drying mutton like prosciutto, it was something we couldn't wait to try. Most good butchers will be able to source you mutton to air-dry, but you may have to wait a while to get a good-quality cut.

Serves 4

500 g (1 pound) lamb neck fillet, whole
6 slices of air-dried mutton

For the root broth
olive oil
1 large onion, chopped
2 carrots, finely diced

2-3 large potatoes, cut into 1 cm (½-inch) dice
250 g (9 ounces) pearl barley (about 375 ml/
1½ cups)
1 large sprig fresh thyme
1.2 L (5 cups) chicken stock

For the marinade
15 ml (1 tablespoon) chopped fresh mint
5 ml (1 teaspoon) fresh thyme leaves
zest and juice of 1 lemon
2 garlic cloves, finely chopped
125 ml (½ cup) white wine
15 ml (1 tablespoon) olive oil
1 pinch salt and freshly ground black pepper

For the garnish
1-2 slices of air-dried mutton
5 ml (1 teaspoon) chopped fresh mint

LAMB WRAPPED IN AIR-DRIED MUTTON WITH ROOT BROTH

Put the lamb fillet in a bowl and add all the marinade ingredients. Cover with plastic wrap, put into the fridge and leave to marinate for as long as you can; 3–4 hours will really make a difference to the taste, but if you're short of time, just rub the marinade into the meat.

To make the broth, heat a little oil in a pan, add the vegetables and cook for 5 minutes. Add the pearl barley and thyme, stir and add the stock. Simmer for 30–40 minutes or until the pearl barley is tender.

Preheat your oven to 240°C (475°F). When you are ready to cook the lamb fillet, take it out of the bowl, reserving the marinade. Wrap the slices of air-dried mutton around the fillet, securing them with toothpicks if necessary. Place the wrapped fillet on a nonstick baking sheet and use a brush to paint the air-dried mutton with the leftover marinade. Cook in the oven for 6–8 minutes, remove, cover with foil and set aside to rest for 3–4 minutes.

When the lamb and broth are both ready, make the garnish. Cut the air-dried mutton into fine strips and heat in a dry frying pan. Slice the wrapped lamb fillet into equal-sized disks and serve on top of a ladleful of broth in wide-rimmed bowls. Garnish with the fried air-dried mutton and chopped mint.

METHOD #10

SALAMI

Sausages are an invaluable way of processing large amounts of lower quality meat, but their shelf-life is short unless they are stored in the freezer. What's the answer? Cure the meat and make air-dried salami instead. The number one benefit in making salami is that it lasts for months and stays fresh because of the curing process. And salami is absolutely delicious. Originally, salami was made only from pork, but other meats, including beef, can also be used. For our salami we like to use a fairly fatty cut of pork, such as shoulder, but any part of the pig will work. The addition of cured pork fat is essential, and you can either cure your own (see pages 46-47) or buy it ready-cured. Because the fat will cure at a different rate from the fresh pork in the rest of the salami, it gives the curing process a head start and means you'll end up with perfection.

PREPARING THE MEAT

If you have a meat grinder, start by cutting your pork into 2.5-cm (1-inch) dice – roughly big enough to be squeezed through the grinder. If you don't have a grinder, don't worry – just buy some ground pork from your local butcher. We started sausage-making years ago, long before we even kept pigs, and used a traditional hand-powered gadget. It was seriously hard work, and we have upgraded to an electric grinder now. It makes the whole process very quick and easy.

As well as dicing the pork meat, you also need to dice the pork fat into 1-cm (½-inch) cubes. These will not only provide the distinctive texture and speckled look to the cut rounds of salami but will also help with the curing process. Do not put the pork fat through the grinder, though – it should go into the mixing bowl as chunky little cubes.

ADDING FLAVOR

Adding herbs and spices to your salami is definitely the creative part. Use herbs that are really aromatic and a bold pepper or spice that can work its way through the salty meat. There are lots of different styles of salami, and our favorites are on page 86, but there are lots more to try once you're confident.

• German – Juniper berries and lots of black pepper make this perfect for a rustic lunch, served with bread and a pint of beer.

• Garlic saucisson – Adding huge amounts of garlic to the mix results in an intense salami that can stand out among an array of other flavors in stews, stuffing or mixed platters.

• Longaniza – A highly seasoned Spanish sausage flavored with hot peppers and fennel that goes particularly well with egg dishes.

PREPARING THE CURE

The difference with salami is that the cure is mixed into the meat, rather than being applied to the exterior. Use at least 2% weight of salt to meat and mix it well. You want the salt to penetrate all the pork, and this is where a salami either succeeds or fails. Table salt is the most economic choice, but you can try other types of salt.

PREPARING TO FILL THE CASINGS

Our sausage-making machine has paid for itself many times over. Every year we make a selection of sausages and salami and they always make us smile when we eat them. Making them is pretty good fun too. It's hard not to enjoy the change from flavored ground meat to uniform sausage. If you don't have a sausage-making machine, don't let that stop you from giving it a try. Use a large funnel and a spatula to force the ground meat through the pipe and into the casings.

We opt for natural casings because we think they are better. They have thousands of years of tradition behind them, they make use of a waste product from the meat industry and the skin of the intestine breathes better than artificial casings, allowing smoked flavors or cooking ingredients to penetrate the salami and infuse it with flavor.

FILLING THE CASINGS

Keep your casings moist, in a bowl of water, and wet them as you put them onto the funnel. You need to use your thumb and forefinger to roll the entire casing onto the funnel. Keep a few centimeters (about an inch) of it overhanging so that you can squeeze out any air bubbles. As you pinch the end of the casing and start to feed the salami mix through, use the other hand to evenly guide the sausage shape.

When you have reached the desired length – normally 20–30 cm (8–12 inches) – stop, pinch the place where you want to tie the casing off and twist the sausage. Use some string to make a knot and then start the process again and continue until you have used up all your salami mix.

HANGING YOUR SALAMI

Use a sharp knife to separate the salamis once you've tied them off. Hang them in a well-ventilated, covered area and leave for a month. During the hanging process the salami ferments, and because of this it has many natural health benefits. For example, it contains lactic acid, which can help maintain a healthy digestive system.

FINISHING THEM OFF

If there is any white mold on the salami, clean them with a vinegar and water solution and a piece of muslin or cheesecloth. They are then ready to slice and serve.

HOW TO MAKE SALAMI

A TRIO OF SALAMI

Every salami contains the same proportion of meat, fat and salt. Add your choice of herbs and spices to the basic recipe or make a classic chorizo or pepperoni. Follow the instructions opposite to prepare.

Makes 15-20 salami

Basic salami

4 kg (9 pounds) pork

1 kg (2 pounds) cured pork fat

100g (3½ ounces) salt (about 125 ml/½ cup)

flavorings (optional)

Chorizo flavorings

30 ml (2 tablespoons) fennel seeds

30 ml (2 tablespoons) smoked paprika

8 garlic cloves, finely chopped

125 ml (½ cup) red wine

Pepperoni flavorings

25 g (1 oz) sugar

30 ml (2 tablespoons) cayenne pepper

30 ml (2 tablespoons) paprika

15 ml (1 tablespoon) crushed fennel seeds

2 garlic cloves, finely crushed

Pepperoni is a mixture of pork and beef. Instead of 4 kg (9 pounds) pork, use 3 kg (6½ pounds) pork and 1 kg (2 pounds) lean beef.

Start by cutting your pork into 2.5 cm (1 inch) dice. Then dice the pork fat into 1-cm (½-inch) cubes. You can use a meat grinder to chop the pork, but dice the pork fat by hand.

Pinch the place where you want to tie off the casing and twist the sausage. Use some string to make a knot.

Put the diced pork and pork fat in a large bowl and add the salt and any flavorings to the mixture.

Moisten your casing and put it on to the funnel. Then feed the salami mix into the casing, using your hand to evenly guide the sausage shape.

Repeat steps 3 and 4 until you have used all your mixture or run out of casings.

Hang your salami in a well-ventilated area under cover and leave for 1 month.

Pizza comes in a staggering number of variations, but without a doubt one of the very best is the simple salami pizza. It's great if you have a pizza stone or special pizza pan, to make sure that the pizza has a crispy base, but, fear not, the pizzas are equally tasty cooked on a baking sheet.

Makes 2 pizzas, about 30 cm (12 inches) in diameter

For the pizza base

1 (7 g/¼-ounce) package dried yeast

2 ml (½ teaspoon) sugar

200 ml (about ⅞ cup) warm water

300 g (10 ounces) flour (about 625 ml/2½ cups)

5 ml (1 teaspoon) salt

For the tomato sauce

extra virgin olive oil, for frying

1 onion, finely diced

2 garlic cloves, crushed

1 (425 g/15-ounce) can tomatoes

10 sun-dried tomatoes, finely chopped

salt and freshly ground black pepper

For the topping

salami slices

20 black olives

grated cheese

SALAMI PIZZA

Mix the yeast, sugar and water in a bowl and set aside for 10 minutes.

Sift the flour and salt into a large bowl. Add the yeast mixture and mix well. Flour a work surface and knead the dough for about 5 minutes, then place it in a greased bowl and cover loosely with plastic wrap. Leave in a warm place to rise for about 1 hour.

To make the tomato sauce, heat a little extra virgin olive oil in a pan and add the onions and garlic. Cook until softened, then add the canned and sun-dried tomatoes and cook gently for about 20 minutes more. Pass the sauce through a sieve, and season with salt and pepper. Set aside.

Once the dough has risen, preheat your oven to 200°C (400°F). Divide the dough in half, then flour a work surface and roll out each half to a circle of at least 30 cm (12 inches) in diameter. Spread each circle with the tomato sauce, and then top with slices of salami, black olives and a little grated cheese. Bake for 15 minutes or until the base is crispy.

There are times when a sweet and spicy meat snack is in order, and on such an occasion we often serve one of our air-dried chorizo sausages. It's a good pre-dinner snack and also happens to taste great with a glass of wine. This quick recipe is our twist on a traditional Spanish tapa dish, and one of the best things about it is that it takes just a few minutes to prepare.

Serves 4

1 large chorizo sausage

3 garlic cloves, peeled

20 ml (1 generous tablespoon) honey

30 ml (2 tablespoons) red wine vinegar

30 ml (2 tablespoons) red wine (optional)

fresh bread, to serve

CHORIZO TAPA WITH HONEY, WINE & GARLIC

Slice the chorizo sausage into 1 cm (½-inch) thick rounds and place them in a hot, nonstick frying pan. Spread out the slices so they are all in one layer and let them sizzle on high heat until the richly colored oils start to ooze out of the meat.

Add the garlic cloves to the pan and turn the chorizo slices over. When you've turned them all over and they are starting to brown and caramelize, add the honey and the red wine vinegar. Add the red wine as well, if you like, to soften the acidity of the vinegar. Keep moving the chorizo around the pan so the sauce doesn't burn. Remove from the heat once the sauce starts to thicken and become sticky.

Serve while still warm with chunks of fresh bread.

This slow-cooked winter warmer is a family favorite. The beef shin becomes amazingly succulent with long, slow cooking, and the flavors in the chorizo infuse the juices so that no extra flavoring is required. We cook this on top of our wood-burning stove, but you can use a slow cooker if you have one. This meaty stew is delicious served with green beans.

Serves 4

1.5 kg (3 pounds) beef shin

300 g (10 ounces) chorizo sausage

75-90 ml (5-6 tablespoons) extra virgin olive oil

3 onions, roughly sliced

4 garlic cloves, sliced

10 ml (2 teaspoons) fennel seeds

2 sprigs fresh rosemary

45 ml (3 tablespoons) all-purpose flour

1 bottle of red wine (or you can use half wine, half stock)

salt and freshly ground black pepper

For the dumplings

100 g (3½ ounces) self-rising flour (about 175 ml/¾ cup)

50 g (2 ounces) suet

7 ml (½ tablespoon) chopped fresh rosemary

salt and freshly ground black pepper

about 45 ml (3 tablespoons) water

BEEF & CHORIZO WITH DUMPLINGS

Cut the beef into 2–3 cm (1 inch) cubes. Cut the chorizo into 1.5 cm (¾-inch) slices.

Heat the oil in a casserole-type pan until very hot. Add the pieces of beef and let them brown in the oil; don't be tempted to stir them too much, as you want to seal the surface and stirring will prevent this from happening. Once they've browned a bit, add the onions and garlic and stir, scraping up the meaty goodness from the bottom of the pan. Cook for 3–4 minutes, then add the chorizo, fennel seeds and rosemary sprigs and cook for a further 2–3 minutes, stirring occasionally.

Sprinkle the all-purpose flour into the pan and stir so that everything is coated. Cook for a couple of minutes then gradually add the wine, stirring all the time. The liquid should not quite cover the meat at this stage. Cover and cook on a gentle heat for at least 2 hours (if you can leave it for longer it will be even better), stirring occasionally and if necessary adding some stock or water. By the time it has finished cooking the pieces of meat will have reduced in size and the liquid should be covering them completely.

To make the dumplings, mix the dry ingredients in a bowl. Add the water slowly until you can form the mixture into four oval-shaped dumplings; they shouldn't be too sticky. Set the dumplings on top of the liquid for the last 30 minutes of the cooking time.

A fiery, chewy snack

METHOD #11

BEEF JERKY

Dried, gnarly-looking bits of meat are much more
delicious than they sound. Jerky is simply flavored
meat cut into strips and dried. It is the ultimate
portable snack, and for us it goes hand in hand
with a fishing trip or an afternoon walk in the
woods. That said, it's equally at home as a picnic
snack or an everyday treat. Jerky is typically
made from beef but can also be made using the
same method from other red meats, such as goat,
lamb or venison.

PREPARING THE JERKY

The best cuts of beef to use are round steak,
skirt steak, rump roast or flank steak. You
can either hang the jerky to dry for 4 days
in a well-ventilated outdoor space or, for the
quicker option, dry it in a convection oven at
50°C (120°F), with the door slightly ajar to
allow moisture to escape. Place a rack at the
top of the oven and hang the strips of meat
between the bars with toothpicks. Make sure
that you place a large piece of foil underneath
to catch any drips. The jerky is ready to eat
when it is pliable but not brittle. To keep it
fresh, store it in an old tobacco pouch or
other sealed bag.

SERVING IT UP

Serve the jerky with a Tabasco dipping
sauce, made by stirring 10 ml (2 teaspoons) of
Tabasco or chili sauce, 15 ml (1 tablespoon)
of honey, 15 ml (1 tablespoon) of white wine
vinegar and 2 garlic cloves in a small pan
over a low heat until the vinegar reduces and
the sauce starts to thicken. Remove the garlic
before serving.

A MARINADE FOR BEEF JERKY

For 1 kg (2 pounds) flank steak

15 ml (1 tablespoon) honey
250 ml (1 cup) soy sauce
250 ml (1 cup) Worcestershire sauce
1 pinch cayenne
5 ml (1 teaspoon) ground coriander seeds
4 garlic cloves, crushed
30 ml (2 tablespoons) freshly ground
black pepper

HOW TO MAKE BEEF JERKY

Take 1 kg (2 pounds) of steak and trim off any fat, as this will not dry well. Then freeze the beef until ice crystals start to form, which will make it much easier to slice thinly.

Next, start work on the marinade. Mix together all of the ingredients (see opposite) in a bowl and then set aside.

Cut the beef into thin slices. Add to the marinade and pour everything into a container with a lid or a resealable plastic bag. Seal and refrigerate for 2 days, turning occasionally.

Remove the beef from the marinade and pat dry with papertowels. Then dry it in a convection oven at 50°C (120°F) with the door slightly ajar; jerky can dry in just 4 hours.

4
HOT SMOKING

HOT SMOKING

Hot smoking cooks cured food for immediate consumption, although the shelf life can be prolonged by vacuum-packing or freezing. Many hot-smoked foods, such as chicken, duck and salmon, make great cold dishes and salads, but hot-smoked food is best eaten as soon as it's ready. There are two elements in hot smoking food - the clue being in the name.

HOW HOT SMOKING WORKS

Cured meat is cooked and flavored by being exposed to hot wood smoke. Different types of wood have their own characteristic flavors, ranging from mild and delicate to dense and pungent. Hot smoking dries out the surface of the meat, and the smoke therefore does not penetrate it completely.

GUIDELINES

- Use the freshest meat or fish.
- Cure the meat or fish before smoking.
- The lower the smoke temperature, the better the smoke diffusion, and the longer the smoking time, the better the taste.
- The higher the smoke temperature, the shorter the smoking time and the shorter the shelf life of the final product.
- Don't allow smoking to take place between 25°C and 60°C (75–140°F), these are temperatures at which microbes can grow to potentially dangerous levels.
- Apart from the danger range, don't fret about the exact temperature – meat is usually hot-smoked at temperatures in the 95–120°C (200–250°F) range, but as it is a matter of personal taste, everyone's advice is slightly different. However, cooking at too high a temperature will change the look, taste and texture of the meat.
- Don't rush the smoking or you will lose the flavor.
- Don't use charcoal impregnated with chemicals to light the smoker.

TEMPERATURE CONTROL

The meat actually cooks in the hot gases from your heat source, which can be gas, electric, charcoal (usually in a barbecue/smoker combination) or even an open fire. Cooking temperatures are generally lower than those used in a conventional oven, which ensures that hot smoking is always a slow-cooking process, allowing the wood flavor to infuse the meat. This form of cooking is sometimes referred to as "low and slow." Cooking at these lower temperatures – 95–120°C (200–250°F) – means that it will take a bit longer to cook the food, hence the "slow." Indeed, cooking the food can take anywhere from 2 to 24 hours, but one of the advantages of slow-cooking is that cheaper cuts of meat can become tender, succulent meals. Use a suitable thermometer to check your smoker is at the desired temperature.

SMOKE

The wood used to create the characteristic smoky flavor is gently heated to promote smoldering rather than burning. Usually the

A combination of heat and smoke is the key

Smoked oysters are delicious

entire hot-smoking process is enclosed, so there are little if any drying effects during the slow-cooking approach. That said, putting a container of water in the smoker can help keep the moisture levels high.

Many commercially available hot-smokers include a water bowl and are therefore also known as water-smokers. The water bowl not only adds moisture to the smoking process, but it also acts as a buffer between the heat source and the food to be smoked, keeping the temperature down. Soaking wood chips in water for an hour before smoking will produce a similar temperature-regulating effect. The added advantage of water-smokers is that you can influence the flavors by using a liquid of your choice – any combination of stock, wine, beer, spices and herbs.

It is a matter of personal choice, but we tend not to water-smoke as we enjoy the traditional textures of our hot-smoked meats. We have been educated that moist meat is a sign of quality, but it is worth considering that the loss of weight actually means that the flavors are concentrated. Smoked meats can lose up to 10% of their moisture during the smoking process. This depends on the temperature, the length of the smoking, the air flow and the humidity in the smokehouse. Eliminating moisture is particularly important when the products are cold-smoked for preservation purposes rather than hot-smoked for flavor and immediate consumption.

The longer the smoking time the bigger the loss of moisture, resulting in a higher proportion of salt. The product becomes drier and saltier but has a much better shelf life. A supply of fresh air is needed during smoking, which is normally controlled with a damper. Exiting smoke also needs a damper control, otherwise tar and other unburned wood particles may start to accumulate, affecting the look and taste of the product.

CREATIVE COMBINATIONS

The scope for hot smoking is very wide: fish, fowl and meat can be mixed with any suitable smoke, allowing for many different flavor combinations and varieties. The trick is to serve your smoked products with accompaniments that complement the flavors you have achieved. You can follow the recipes in this chapter or use them as inspiration for cooking whatever you have smoked.

SAFETY!

When you are smoking meat or fish it is important that the temperature you keep the food at is out of the range that is ideal for bacterial growth. The really dangerous area is near our body temperature, as that is when bacteria thrive and grow very quickly. As a rule of thumb, never cook food in temperatures between 25°C and 60°C (75–140°F).

CHOOSING WOOD FOR YOUR SMOKER

WOOD	CHARACTERISTICS	USES
Alder	Very delicate	Fish and poultry
Apple	Slightly sweet but relatively dense	Red meats and cheeses
Ash	Fast burner with delicate, unique flavor	Fish
Birch	Mild	Pork and poultry
Cherry	Slightly sweet	Meats
Chestnut	Nutty	Cheeses
Hickory	Pungent and dense	All
Maple	Similar to birch	Cheeses and poultry
Mesquite	Strong and dense	Red meats
Oak	Heavy smoke flavor	All
Pear	Slightly sweet	Cheeses and poultry

METHOD #12

HOT-SMOKERS

Having your own hot-smoker is an incredible luxury that will give you years of service and provide countless opportunities for delicious meals. Buying a smoker is easy -- just have a look online -- but we found it more satisfying to build our own, using a mixture of old unused items and new ones bought especially for the smoker, like the timber for the smoke box. Site your hot-smoker in a shed or other outbuilding, well away from flammable material, and always keep a close eye on it when in use, adjusting the heat and flame as you work.

CHOOSING A SMOKER

Commercially available hot-smokers tend to fall into two categories: those for use in the kitchen (stove-top or electric) and outdoor barbecue/water-smokers. The range of water-smokers available commercially is staggering, but basically they all have a heat source, a pan for water and a rack for the meat. The lid provides a good seal, but the air flow that controls the temperature of the charcoal and the density of the smoke is usually adjustable with simple sliding vents.

MAKING A LARGE SMOKER

As with a store-bought hot-smoker, you need a controllable source of heat and a means of generating smoke. We designed a smoker that is capable of both hot smoking and cold smoking and has significant temperature control (see the diagram opposite).

The smoke generator is an old wood-burning stove that has no doors. A piece of plywood provides the necessary seal/door and a 12-volt fan from a computer keeps the

sawdust, our chosen source of smoke, smoldering. We use a blowtorch to light it, which if held still for about 20 seconds provides a strong ember. A piece of flexible ducting connects the smoke box to the smoke chamber. This separation allows the smoke to cool and also lets any sediment settle in the ducts. For cold smoking that's all you need – it's just a matter of putting what you wish to smoke into the smoke box and adjusting the air flow. We drilled holes in the top of our smoke box, which are plugged by corks from wine bottles. The number of holes we leave open determines the air flow and therefore the density of the smoke.

To use the smoke box as a hot-smoker we have a gas ring in the bottom with a piece of metal (copper in our case) that sits above it and spreads the heat. Adjusting the temperature is not very complicated – it's just a matter of varying the gas flow. It may seem a bit risky to have a gas ring in a wooden box, but the temperatures we are smoking at are not severe, since we keep it "low and slow."

SAFETY!

It is important to keep safety in mind when using your hot-smoker. Check that all the equipment is in good working order before you start and do not leave the smoker unattended for long periods of time.

Keep the smoke in

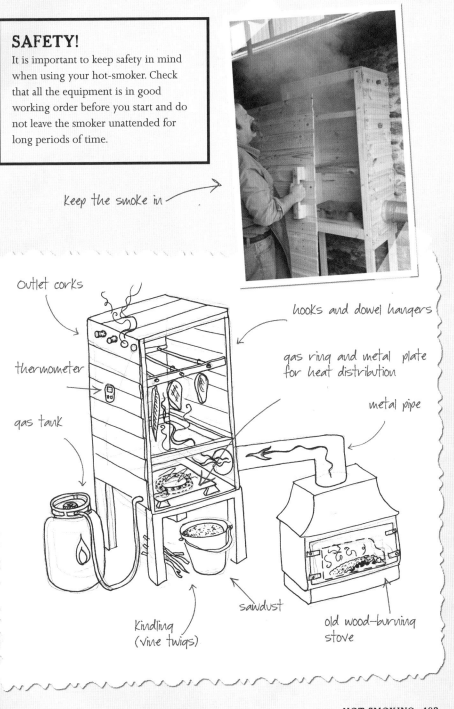

Outlet corks

hooks and dowel hangers

thermometer

gas ring and metal plate for heat distribution

metal pipe

gas tank

sawdust

Kindling (vine twigs)

old wood-burning stove

PREPARING MEAT & FISH

- Fish – Fillet and remove the pin bones or cure whole, with salt rubbed into the cavity.
- Chicken & turkey – Fillet and cut into portions or smoke whole. If smoked whole, the skin around the neck end should be trimmed off and the neck removed completely so there is a good flow of smoke through the cavity. If just the thighs or the thickest part of the breast are being smoked, pierce several times with a skewer so that the salt can enter the flesh.
- Duck – Trim the skin from the neck end and prick lots of holes into the flesh prior to curing. If just the breast is being smoked, this also needs to be pricked.
- Beef, pork, lamb & mutton – Bone or fillet the meat. It is useful if it can be cut to a uniform thickness, as this makes the cooking even throughout. Trim off any loose fat.

CURING YOUR MEAT OR FISH

Curing can be dry (see page 42–45) or wet (see pages 18–21), adding the flavors you think complement the meat. Alternatively, a simple salt and sugar cure will allow the flavor of the meat to stand alone. The meat should be stored in the fridge or a cool place for the duration of the curing.

Once the curing has finished, the excess salt needs to be removed. Briefly rinse the meat in cold water, pat dry with papertowels and then allow to dry completely. This can be done in a cool, dry place or even in an oven with the fan on and the heat off. When drying is complete there may be a dried sugar/salt crust left on the flesh – this is called a pellicle and it is does not need to be removed. Make sure that the meat is dry before moving to the hot-smoking stage.

CURING FOR SMOKING

PRODUCT	CURE TIMES (HOURS)	COMMENTS
Side of salmon	1	Dry cure
Mackerel	½	Dry cure
Trout fillet	¼	Dry cure
Duck breast	1	Dry cure
	3	Brine
Whole duck	6	Dry cure
	12	Brine
Chicken	4	Dry cure
	8	Brine
Beef	12	Dry cure
	24	Brine
Pork	9	Dry cure
	18	Brine

PREPARING THE SMOKER

It is best to allow your smoker to reach equilibrium before you open it and add the meat. If you are using a water pan, you should add hot liquid rather than waiting for your smoker to heat it up from cold.

SMOKING MEAT & FISH

Cooking times are estimates at best (see the chart opposite). However, the best and most accurate way of testing that the meat is cooked is with a good-quality meat thermometer, which will measure the internal temperature of the food being cooked.

During hot smoking, the texture of the

TIMING & TEMPERATURES

It doesn't matter how clever you think you are about controlling the temperature of your hot-smoker, there will be some variation over time if you have a fire to keep stoked or smoke to be generated at a constant rate from smoldering sawdust or chippings. With all these variables, and of course the variation in the size and shape of your meat, you will find you end up in the realm of guestimation when it comes to cooking times.

The cooking times below are only a guide, and as long as the recommended internal temperatures are achieved all will be well.

PRODUCT	APPROXIMATE SMOKING/ COOKING TIME	INTERNAL TEMPERATURE WHEN COOKED
Beef sirloin roast	3–4 hours	Rare 50°C (120°F) Medium 60°C (140°F) Well done 70°C (160°F)
Beef brisket	6–8 hours	85°C (185°F)
Beef rib roast	6–18 hours	Rare 50°C (120°F) Medium 60°C(140°F) Well done 70°C (160°F)
Whole chicken	3½–4 hours	75°C (170°F)
Chicken breast or thigh	45 minutes	75°C (170°F)
Whole turkey	8 hours	75°C (170°F)
Whole duck	3–4 hours	65°C (150°F)
Duck breast	1 hour	65°C (150°F)
Pork shoulder	12+ hours	85–90°C (185–195°F)
Pork loin	4–5 hours	65°C (150°F)
Pork ribs	5–6 hours	Cook until the meat comes away from the bone easily
Whole salmon	2–3 hours	Cook until the flesh flakes easily
Side of salmon	45 minutes	Cook until the flesh flakes easily
Shrimp	20 minutes	Cook until they become bright pink

food will become softer and less dense. For fish, for example hot-smoked salmon, the flesh will flake when pulled apart. Poultry is smoked for less time than red meat, and as it has skin the surface should be colored but the flesh still remain pale. After hot smoking a cut of meat and getting it to the stage of being done or even well done, you should be able to carve the meat and see a dark red color caused by the smoking process. This does not run deep under the surface (but the deeper the better).

FINISHING IT OFF

When your food comes out of the smoker it is ready to eat – indeed, oysters must be eaten immediately – but most meats will benefit from being allowed to stand. Once cooled, put the meat in the fridge for a couple of hours or, if possible, overnight.

Hot–smoked duck breasts

SMOKED EEL

Smoked eel is a real delicacy. It used to be a very common dish, but with dwindling eel numbers it is becoming harder to find. If you can buy or catch fresh eel, it is definitely worth considering smoking it. Remove the guts by cutting the underbelly and clean out with papertowels. Cure the eel in brine for 2 hours to dry it out, then rinse it and pat it dry. Place toothpicks or short bits of wooden barbecue skewer inside to hold the belly cavity apart – this will allow the smoke to really penetrate the flesh and fill it with powerfully fragrant wood flavors.

SMOKING ON YOUR STOVE TOP

It takes moments to rustle up hot-smoked pigeon breast or smoked trout in a stove-top smoker. The principles are very simple: it is basically a pan with a lid and a rack inside on which you put the meat to be hot smoked. The smoking material, usually wood chips, is put on the bottom of the pan. When the pan is heated the air inside becomes very hot and the wood heats up and begins to smolder. The meat is cooked by the hot air and the smoke infuses the meat. The system is quite difficult to regulate, and the heat inside can become quite fierce. (See hot-smoked pigeon breast, pages 120–121.)

MAKING A STOVE-TOP SMOKER

You can make your own stove-top smoker for smaller cuts of fish or meat from things usually found in the kitchen.

A large steel pan is lined with foil on which you place the smoking material. The foil protects the pan. Place a rack in the pan above the smoking material; we cut a cake-cooling rack to size, but if you have a little rack that fits, that's perfect.

lid   foil folded up

fish

metal rack

wood chips (rice, tea or sugar can also be used)

PASTRAMI

Pastrami is actually cured beef brisket cooked in spices, hot smoked and then steam cooked. Making your own pastrami is a fairly time-consuming process. However, once you've tasted the homemade version, you'll find that store bought pastrami just doesn't compare. Our recipe gives a pastrami that is both sweet and spicy, smoky and succulent.

PREPARING THE BRISKET

Follow the brined brisket process (see pages 32–33) and soak for 5 days. Then replace the brine with a sweeter mixture – 400g (13 ounces) each of sugar and salt dissolved in 4 litres (7 pints) of water – for another 5 days. Remove the brisket from the brine and pat it dry with papertowels. Vigorously massage the spice rub mixture into the brisket, trying to get as much to stick to the meat as possible.

HOT SMOKING THE BRISKET

Hot-smoke the brisket to an internal temperature of 70°C (160°F). If it is too hot to comfortably touch, you know you are on track, but if you want to be extra careful you can use a meat thermometer. You can smoke the brisket by cooking it in any covered barbecue. Try to keep the temperature low and steady so that the cooking takes as long as possible, and keep adding handfuls of sawdust or wood chips to the fire to keep it smoky. Arrange the brisket on a piece of heavy-duty foil to reduce direct heat and still allow smoke to circulate. Turn regularly and cook for 2–3 hours with the lid on.

FINISHING IT OFF

Put the smoked brisket on a rack over a deep roasting pan with about an inch of boiling water in the bottom. Build a foil hat around it and pinch the edges together. Keep as much free space around the meat as possible for the steam to circulate. Cook in a preheated oven at 120°C (250°F) for 3 hours. After the allotted time, you should be able to easily slide a fork into the brisket. Once ready, slice the meat thinly across the grain while it's still hot and serve warm, sandwiched between slices of rye bread.

A SPICE RUB FOR PASTRAMI

For 1 kg (2 pounds) beef brisket

45 ml (3 tablespoons) coarsely ground black peppercorns

5 ml (1 teaspoon) crushed garlic

30 ml (2 tablespoons) ground coriander seeds

15 ml (1 tablespoon) smoked paprika

5 ml (1 teaspoon) red pepper flakes

Crush the peppercorns, garlic and coriander seeds with a mortar and pestle, keeping the texture coarse. Add the paprika and chilli flakes.

HOW TO MAKE PASTRAMI

Cure the brisket in brine for 5 days, then replace the brine with a sweeter mixture – equal parts sugar and salt dissolved in water – for a further 5 days. Remove from the brine.

Pat the brisket dry with papertowels and massage the spice rub into the surface of the meat. Hot-smoke the brisket for 2–3 hours, turning it regularly.

Put the smoked brisket on a rack over a deep roasting pan with about an inch of boiling water in the bottom.

Build a foil hat around the roasting pan and seal up by pinching the edges together. Cook in a preheated oven at 120°C (250°F) for 3 hours.

The king-size double-decker sandwich with sauerkraut, pickles and mustard is what made New York delis famous. Our preferred way of serving it is influenced by our time spent living in Germany and a simple love of pickles.

Serves 4

For the sauerkraut
15 ml (1 tablespoon) olive oil
1 onion, thinly sliced
1 cabbage, shredded
310 ml (1⅓ cup) apple cider vinegar
125 ml (½ cup) cider
15 ml (1 tablespoon) salt

For the sandwich
500 g (1 pound) pastrami, thinly sliced
16 mini pickles, sliced
12 slices rye bread
English mustard

PASTRAMI ON RYE

First make the sauerkraut. This is a quick recipe that doesn't take as long as the traditional fermenting method. Heat the oil in a pan then add the onion and cook until it softens. Add the cabbage, vinegar, cider and salt and bring to a boil. Reduce to a simmer and cook for about 30 minutes, adding water if it gets too dry. This simple sauerkraut will keep for 2 weeks in the fridge if stored in a sealed jar.

Use 3 slices of bread and 6–8 slices of pastrami for each sandwich. Spread the first slice of bread with mustard, add a layer of sauerkraut and top with a layer of pastrami and sliced pickles. Repeat this sequence and finish with the third slice of bread.

Spicy and succulent slices

HOT-SMOKED CHICKEN

There's one thing that's certain: if you have a smoked chicken in your fridge it will get eaten, so if you are firing up your smoker it may be worth preparing more than one. Hot smoking a chicken takes a bit of time, but you are mostly waiting for the chicken to cure or to smoke, so it's not really a lot of effort and it is definitely worth the wait. Experiment with the type of wood smoke you use -- we particularly like to use beech or sweet chestnut, but try different types of wood (see page 101) and decide what you like best. If you want to make your smoked chicken last, serve it thinly sliced in salads and so on.

PREPARING THE CHICKEN

First cut the excess skin from the neck and the vent end of the chicken to allow a flow of air through the cavity. It is also sensible to give the bird a good stretch. Simply grab the wings and pull them apart, and then grab the legs and pull them apart also – this will open the chest cavity.

MAKING THE CURE

For a 2 kg (4 pound) chicken, mix together 200 g (7 ounces) of salt (about 250 ml/1 cup), 100g (3½ ounces) of sugar (about 125ml/½ cup) and 10 crushed peppercorns, plus any aromatic spices or herbs you fancy.

CURING YOUR CHICKEN

Rub the inside and outside of the chicken with the cure mixture, then place the chicken in a plastic container. Now pack the rest of the salt mix inside and all over the outside of the chicken, especially in between the legs and on the breast. Put the container in a cool place for at least 4 hours, but you can leave it overnight if you like. When the curing has finished, remove the bird from the cure mix,

rinse off all the salt and dry it thoroughly with papertowels. Put a wooden skewer through the breast, under the wings, and hang it up until it is dry.

HOT SMOKING THE CHICKEN

Start your hot-smoker and get it to about 110°C (225°F) before opening the lid and putting in the chicken. The bird should reach a temperature of 75°C (170°F) within 4 hours. Test it in the thickest part of the thigh and breast.

FINISHING IT OFF

Once smoked, allow the bird to cool before putting it into the fridge. The smoke will continue to permeate the flesh, so it is always best to leave the bird for another day before eating it – sealing it in a bag before placing it in the fridge will keep the rest of your fridge contents from getting smoky. The smoked chicken can be stored in the fridge for a week.

NOW TRY: DUCK AND TURKEY

These birds can be smoked in the same way as chicken. Try adding cumin, cloves, cinnamon and coriander seeds to the cure mix.

HOW TO HOT SMOKE A CHICKEN

Rub the inside and outside of the chicken with cure mixture then put it in a container. Pack the rest of the salt mix inside and all over the outside of the bird.

Put the container in a cool place for at least 4 hours. When the curing has finished, rinse all the salt off.

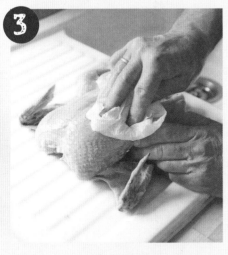

Dry the chicken thoroughly with papertowels. Put a wooden skewer through the breast, under the wings, and hang it up until it is dry.

Start your hot-smoker, and once it reaches 110°C (225°F) put in the chicken. The bird should reach a temperature of 75°C (170°F) within 4 hours. Test it in the thickest part of the thigh and breast.

This dish shows off the smoky undertones of the chicken and balances them with the fresh herbs. It makes a great starter or lunchtime snack and is delicious served with a thick slice of toasted brioche.

Serves 4

For the terrine

800 ml (2 gallons) chicken stock

4 sheets leaf gelatin

10 ml (2 teaspoons) chopped fresh thyme

1 garlic clove, chopped

450 g (15½ ounces) smoked chicken

5 ml (1 teaspoon) chopped fresh chives

30 ml (2 tablespoons) lemon juice

2 egg whites

100 g (3½ ounces) dried apricots, quartered

lime, orange, pink grapefruit or lemon zest, to garnish

For the citrus dressing

juice of 1 lime

juice of 1 orange

juice of ½ pink grapefruit

juice of ½ lemon

30 ml (2 tablespoons) white wine vinegar

10 ml (2 teaspoons) sugar

1 pinch salt

SMOKED CHICKEN TERRINE

Heat half the chicken stock in a pan and stir in the gelatine until dissolved. Set aside. Put the rest of the stock in another pan, add the thyme and garlic and bring to a boil. Then reduce the heat and add the gelatine and stock from the first pan. Set aside until cooled, but don't allow the stock to reach setting point.

Line a loaf pan with plastic wrap, then spoon in some of the stock and gelatin mix to create a thin layer on the base.

Put the smoked chicken, chives, lemon juice and the rest of the thyme in a food processor. Whisk the egg whites, add them to the processor and whiz to small chunks. Spread a layer of chopped apricots in the pan, followed by a layer of the smoked chicken mixture, then add more stock. Follow this with a second layer of chopped apricots and then another layer of chicken. Repeat until everything is used up, adding more stock at each stage. Refrigerate for 2–3 hours or until set.

To make the citrus dressing, whisk all the ingredients together and pour into a clean bottle or jar.

Turn the terrine out of the pan, using the plastic wrap lining to help you. Serve in slices, surrounded by pea shoots, drizzled with the citrus dressing and sprinkled with a little zest.

It's not often that there is any leftover breast meat when we hot-smoke chicken -- it's usually the first thing that's eaten. This dish makes the breast go a long way, as it's rather rich.

Serves 4

250 g (9 ounces) smoked chicken breast
60 ml (¼ cup) mayonnaise
30 ml (2 tablespoons) lemon juice
5 ml (1 teaspoon) Dijon mustard

For the phyllo cups
6 sheets phyllo pastry
butter

SMOKED CHICKEN MOUSSE

Coarsely dice the chicken breast and put it in a food processor. Whiz for about 20 seconds, then add the mayonnaise, lemon juice and mustard and continue to process for about 1 minute, until the mixture becomes a smooth mousse. Halfway through, scrape down the sides of the processor so everything is blended together, adding a little cold water to loosen the mixture if necessary. Transfer the mixture to a small bowl and chill in the fridge.

Meanwhile, heat the oven to 180°C (350°F), and grease a muffin pan with a little butter. Cut the phyllo pastry into triangles that will fit into the cups in your muffin pan and allow the points to overhang by about 2cm (¾ inch); the sides of your triangles should be about 20 cm (8 inches) long. You will need three triangles per cup. Brush the phyllo triangles with melted butter and place them in the muffin cups, pressing them down gently and overlapping the edges so that the tips of the triangles form a "flower."

Bake for about 6 minutes or until golden brown. Allow to cool in the pan, then remove carefully and set aside.

Spoon the chilled chicken mousse into the phyllo cups and serve topped with a few salad leaves.

Two duck and citrus salads in one book? We couldn't resist. When you first taste duck meat that's been gently smoked you'll wonder why you've been wasting so much time eating it any other way. This is one of our simplest recipes but also one of the tastiest. We like to use blood oranges for their color and their piquant taste, but any old orange will work.

Serves 2

For the salad

2 smoked duck breasts

1 large blood orange (if you can get it, otherwise use an ordinary orange)

2–3 handfuls mixed salad leaves

5 ml (1 teaspoon) orange zest

6–12 fresh rosemary flowers (optional)

For the dressing

5 ml (1 teaspoon) orange juice

10 ml (2 teaspoons) olive oil

1 pinch salt and freshly ground black pepper

HOT-SMOKED DUCK SALAD

Put each duck breast on a chopping board and slice at an angle, cutting across the grain and keeping the slices about 5 mm (¼ inch) thick.

Peel the orange, leaving as little white pith as possible, then cut it into segments.

Arrange the salad leaves in a serving dish and scatter the slices of smoked duck on top. Scatter with orange zest and a sprinkle of rosemary flowers if you've got them.

Whisk together the dressing ingredients and drizzle over the salad.

HOT-SMOKED PIGEON BREAST

Pigeon is a rich, earthy meat that takes hot smoking extremely well, and it's a great introduction to game for anyone who hasn't tried it before. Even if you don't have access to fresh pigeon, you can buy frozen pigeon breasts from most butchers, and they will work just as well.

PREPARING THE PIGEON

Pigeon breasts are not very big, but 1½ per person will be more than enough. Because pigeon breasts are small, they don't need a full cure – just an hour sitting in a good grind of salt and pepper and any other seasoning you would like to add.

PREPARING THE SMOKER

Put a couple of spoonfuls of wood shavings in the base of your smoker and light them, then put the rack in place and leave the lid partially open. Turn on the heat to full and wait until the smoke starts to flow.

SMOKING YOUR PIGEON

When the smoke is ready, put the pigeon breasts in the smoker and close the lid. Turn the heat down to medium. The shavings will probably last for 4 or 5 minutes, so after 4 minutes turn off the heat and leave the breasts in the smoker for another 4 minutes. Stove-top smokers are hard to control precisely, so it is best to infuse the meat and cook it a minimum amount of time so it does not dry out.

FINISHING IT OFF

Once smoked, the breasts will be rare and should be eaten right away. The meat can bear heating in a sauce that provides moisture and maximizes the flavors.

NOW TRY: RABBIT

The lean meat of rabbit can be smoked in the same way as pigeon breast. Don't smoke

Rare, moist and smoky

the rabbit for any longer as the small cuts of meat will start to dry out. When dressing your rabbit and preparing to smoke it, the best option is to take the meat off the bone. The loin is the most tender cut, and it should not be cooked too much or it can go tough.

It is not usual to serve rabbit pink or rare, so after smoking the meat it is a good idea to cook it further. You could do this by cooking the smoked rabbit in a sauce or a pie.

NOW TRY: SMALL GAME BIRDS
Some smaller game birds have a very delicate flavor and need only a light smoking. Pheasant is probably the most widely available game bird. The breast needs to be cut into about three pieces before smoking.

HOW TO HOT SMOKE PIGEON BREASTS

Put a couple of spoonfuls of wood shavings in the base of your smoker and light them.

Put the rack in place and leave the lid partially open. Turn the heat on full, and when the smoke starts to flow put in the pigeon breasts and close the lid.

Turn the heat down to medium. After 4 minutes turn off the heat and leave the breasts in the smoker for another 4 minutes.

Pigeon is an earthy, rich meat that takes hot smoking extremely well and is magnificent with fungi, cream and sherry. The pigeon should be just cooked or it can become tough, so serve as soon as the dish has been brought together and while the cream is warm.

Serves 4

1 small package store-bought puff pastry

1 egg, beaten with a little milk

25 g (1 ounce) butter (about 30 ml/2 tablespoons)

1 small onion, diced

2 garlic cloves, finely chopped

250 g (½ pound) mixed mushrooms, sliced

150 ml (⅔ a cup) sherry

8 hot-smoked pigeon breasts, sliced

250 ml (1 cup) heavy cream (36%)

sea salt and freshly ground black pepper

fresh thyme, to garnish

SMOKED PIGEON & MUSHROOM PIE

Preheat the oven to 180°C (350°F).

Roll out the puff pastry and cut out four circles 10 cm (4 inches) in diameter. Put them on a baking sheet, brush them with the beaten egg and milk and bake for 20 minutes or until golden.

Meanwhile, heat the butter in a pan and add the onion and garlic. Cook gently until soft and transparent, and then add the mushrooms and cook until they start to soften. Turn up the heat and add the sherry. Let it bubble for 2 minutes, and then add the pigeon and the cream. Season with salt and pepper. When it is warm it is ready to serve.

Spoon the sauce onto plates and top each serving with a puff pastry disk. Garnish with thyme and serve with green beans.

METHOD #16

HOT-SMOKED MACKEREL

Hot smoking is a sure way to infuse the aromatic flavor right into the depth of your mackerel. The bonus is that not only does it help to preserve fish for a little longer, but it also cooks them so they are ready to eat. Whether you use a large home-made smoker or opt for a stove-top version, the principles are the same. And you can use the same method for fresh eel. Home-smoked mackerel is nothing like the solid, rather hard fillets that you find vacuum-packed in supermarkets. When you smoke your own mackerel you will find it is very succulent and moist. This makes it a pleasure to eat simply on it own as well as using it as an ingredient in other dishes.

PREPARING THE MACKEREL

Using a filleting knife, take the fillets off by cutting in behind the gills, towards the spine and then, in a smooth cut, follow the line of the bones across the length of the fish towards the tail. Before you reach the tail, bring the knife up to separate the fillet, then flip over the fish and repeat for the other side. When finished, clean off any excess blood and guts with papertowels.

DRYING THE MACKEREL

If you are smoking the mackerel in order to store it for longer, dry out the fillets before smoking. Drying the mackerel can be done in a simple brine solution or by leaving them in some dry table salt for an hour. For a brine solution, mix 1 L (4 cups) of water with 100 g (3½ ounces) of salt (about 125 ml/ ½ cup) and 50 g (2 ounces) of sugar (about 60 ml/¼ cup) in a large saucepan. Heat until the salt and sugar have dissolved then allow the brine to cool. Cover the mackerel in cooled brine and leave in the fridge for 30 minutes. Then remove the fish from the brine and pat dry with papertowels.

PREPARING THE SMOKER

Put 110 g (3¾ ounces) of loose tea leaves (preferably Earl Grey or jasmine), 250 g (9 ounces) of short-grain rice (about 310 ml/1¼ cups) and 30 ml (2 tablespoons) of sugar in the bottom of your stove-top smoker.

SMOKING YOUR MACKEREL

Put the fish on a small rack above the tea, rice and sugar. Always position the fillets so that you can see the flesh, with the skin away from you. The color will serve as an indicator of how smoky they will taste. Place the lid on the smoker and then fold the foil over. Cook for 5 minutes on high heat and a further 10 minutes on low heat to enjoy your own delicious hot-smoked fish. If smoking in a larger smoker, cook for 30–40 minutes.

FINISHING IT OFF

Generally, we like to allow smoked fish to cool and eat it cold a day later, but there is also something special about a fillet of fish put on a plate straight from the smoker. If you are not going to eat the mackerel right away, refrigerate it and consume within 10 days.

HOW TO HOT-SMOKE MACKEREL

Put the tea leaves, rice and sugar in the bottom of your stove-top smoker.

Place the filleted mackerel, skin side down, on a small rack above the tea, rice and sugar.

Place the lid on the smoker and then fold the foil over.

Cook for 5 minutes on high heat and a further 10 minutes on low heat.

The mackerel is the star of this salad, while the rhubarb relish complements its peppery seasoning and natural oils. Keeping it quick and easy fits with the fish itself, one of the few we readily catch when we go out fishing. You can serve the mackerel at room temperature or even use it warm, straight from the smoker.

Serves 2

1-2 stalks forced rhubarb, chopped

30 ml (2 tablespoons) roughly chopped fresh ginger

150 g (5 ounces) sugar (about 175 ml/¾ cup)

juice and zest of 1 lemon

5 ml (1 teaspoon) cracked black pepper

4 hot-smoked mackerel fillets

1 large bunch fresh arugula

2 spring onions, chopped

5 ml (1 teaspoon) extra virgin olive oil

SMOKED MACKEREL WITH ARUGULA SALAD & RHUBARB RELISH

Start by making the rhubarb relish. Combine the rhubarb, ginger, sugar and most of the lemon juice in a pan and simmer on low heat for about 15 minutes, until the juices have been released. Turn the heat up to medium and cook until the relish starts to thicken.

Meanwhile, sprinkle black pepper generously over the smoked mackerel fillets.

Put the arugula and spring onions in a serving bowl, dress with the olive oil and a dash of lemon juice and top with the lemon zest.

Serve the mackerel with the salad and a spoonful of rhubarb relish.

This is a secret family recipe, making its appearance in public for the first time. Our smoked mackerel pâté has become a summertime staple. We love smoking our own mackerel at home, but the recipe works just as well with store-bought vacuum-packed fillets coated in cracked black pepper.

For the mackerel pâté

500 g (1 pound) smoked mackerel

250 g (9 ounces) crème frâiche or sour cream (about 250 ml/1 cup)

10 ml (2 teaspoons) horseradish sauce

5 ml (1 teaspoon) freshly ground black pepper

10 ml (2 teaspoons) whole grain or Dijon mustard

15 ml (1 tablespoon) lemon juice

brown toast, to serve

For the apple slaw

1 large beet

2 small kohlrabies (purple, if you can get them)

1 apple

15 ml (1 heaping tablespoon) mayonnaise

salt and freshly ground black pepper

SMOKED MACKEREL PÂTÉ WITH APPLE SLAW

Put all the ingredients for the pâté in a bowl and use a fork to mix them together. The pâté can be as smooth as you like, so experiment until you reach your preferred consistency.

Peel and grate the beet. Then peel the kohlrabi and slice it thinly using a mandolin (if you don't have one, grate it like the beet). Peel and core the apple and cut it into slices. Mix everything together in a bowl with the mayonnaise and season with salt and pepper.

Serve the pâté with appleslaw and slices of toast.

Freshwater eel, or unagi, is an ingredient that people often don't know how to cook. This recipe plays to its strengths and retains the delicate flavor without using too many other ingredients. "Nigiri" means "hand shaped," and when it comes to the fine art of sushi this is a great place to start.

Serves 4 (3 rolls per person)

For the sushi rice

150 g (5 ounces) sushi rice (about 175 ml/¾ cup)

75 ml (3 fl ounces) rice vinegar

50 g (2 ounces) sugar (about 60 ml/¼ cup)

30 ml (2 tablespoons) salt

For the horseradish mustard

10 ml (2 teaspoons) grated horseradish

5 ml (1 teaspoon) Dijon mustard

To assemble the nigiri

12 slices smoked eel

12 strips nori (dried seaweed)

30 ml (2 tablespoons) kabayaki sauce, to glaze

15 ml (1 tablespoon) sesame seeds

To serve

pickled ginger

plain soy sauce

UNAGI NIGIRI

Cook the sushi rice according to the instructions on the package. While the rice is cooking, put the vinegar, sugar and salt in a pan. Heat until the sugar dissolves, then set aside to cool. Drain the rice then spread it in a shallow dish and use a fork to separate the grains, slowly adding the vinegar at the same time. Cover the rice with a cloth until ready to use.

Put the grated horseradish and mustard in a bowl and mix to a smooth paste.

To assemble your sushi, first moisten your hands in a bowl of water so that the rice won't stick to them too much, and then shape about 30 ml (2 tablespoons) of the sushi rice into a small oblong about the size of a Ping-Pong ball. Place a slice of eel along the rice (this can be used cold but is normally heated under a grill for a minute or two). Place a strip of nori at a right angle across the rice and eel, pinch it at the sides and then seal the two ends together, underneath, to wrap the rice. Glaze the nori and eel with the kabayaki sauce and sprinkle some sesame seeds on top, then place on a plate and set aside while you make the rest of your unagi nigiri the same way.

When the rolls are all ready, serve with the horseradish mustard, pickled ginger and soy sauce.

HOT-SMOKED OYSTERS

Eaten raw with a drop of lemon juice and a pinch of cayenne pepper, oysters are hard to beat. However, eating oysters raw is not to everyone's taste, and for anyone lucky enough to eat oysters regularly, it's lovely to have a change. If you are feeling adventurous and want to try to preserve your oysters, smoking them is the way forward. You can also use this method to smoke mussels, scallops and cockles.

SHUCKING YOUR OYSTERS

First, you need to open the oysters and put them on ice. This can be hard work, and it is worth investing in a shucking knife, but if you don't have one, use a strong, small knife that you are not worried about breaking. Wear gloves or wrap a tea towel around your hand the first time you shuck an oyster; not only are the shells sharp, but if you're rushing the opening process you could end up stabbing yourself. Don't use too much force, as you may damage the oyster or let the knife slip and hurt yourself.

To open an oyster, hold it firmly in one hand, slide the tip of your blade firmly into the slit between the two valves and wiggle it to ease it in. Twist the knife so there is a popping sound, and then slide the blade upward, toward the muscles that hold the shell shut. Finish off by separating the oyster from the shell with the knife.

PREPARING THE SMOKER

Mix the smoking ingredients in a small bowl. For eight oysters you will need 250 g (9 ounces) of long-grain rice (about 310 ml/1¼ cups), 15–30 ml (1–2 tablespoons) of loose tea (preferably Earl Grey or jasmine) and 250 g (8 ounces) of demerara or light brown sugar. Line a pan with foil leaving an overlap above the top of the pan – use this overlap to seal the lid later. Pour the smoking mixture into the pan and place a small grill (a circular one is ideal if you have one) with another layer of foil on top of it to hold the oysters.

SMOKING YOUR OYSTERS

Place the pan on the heat so that it can start smoking, and when it is puffing away add the oysters. Then put the lid on the pan and press the overlapping foil firmly around the lid to keep as much of the smoke inside as possible. The smoke will infuse the oysters with flavor and cook them. Keep the pan on the heat for 10–15 minutes. Throw away the smoking mixture (it's a good idea to leave it to cool before putting it into the garbage) and serve the oysters immediately or chill for an hour.

SAFETY!

Oysters need to be kept in the fridge and consumed within a couple of days. You should only ever purchase and prepare live oysters, and you'll normally know that they are alive if their shells are tightly shut or they close quickly when you tap them. If they are open and don't respond to the "tapping test," don't eat them.

HOW TO HOT-SMOKE OYSTERS

Mix the sugar, rice and tea together in a little bowl. Then line a pan with foil so that there is an overlap above the top of the pan and pour the smoking mixture into the pan.

Place a circular grill in the pan and put foil on top of the grill to hold the oysters. Place the pan on the heat to start smoking, and when it is smoking add the oysters.

Next place the lid on the pan and use the overlapping foil to seal the smoke in, pressing the foil firmly around the lid.

Keep the pan on the heat for 10–15 minutes. Then throw away the smoking mixture and either leave your oysters to chill or serve them immediately.

We love the contrast of fresh salsa with smoky oysters. The salsa here is simple -- the dish keeps the smoked oysters as the hero and is perfect with a glass of dry white wine on a warm spring night.

Serves 4 people as a snack or 2 as an appetizer

8 smoked oysters

cayenne pepper

chopped fresh cilantro, to garnish

For the salsa

3 large tomatoes

1 garlic clove

1 fresh red chili, seeded

½ red onion

2–4 sprigs fresh cilantro

juice of 1 lime

SMOKED OYSTERS & SALSA

To make the salsa, chop the tomatoes, garlic, chili, onion and cilantro together and sprinkle with the lime juice. Set aside.

Season the chilled oysters with a pinch of cayenne pepper. Place an oyster in each shell and cover with a generous spoonful of the salsa and chopped cilantro. If you can find it at a local fishmarket, a garnish of samphire, or sea asparagus, is a nice touch.

5
COLD
SMOKING

COLD SMOKING

Cold smoking is a means not of cooking but of preserving food, and if kept in cool conditions, cold-smoked products should last for many months. The name, of course, says it all, and it is important to use as little heat as possible. Therein lies the challenge: we all know that there is "no smoke without fire," but we need smoke and we don't want any heat. It sounds tricky, but cold smoking is surprisingly easy and delivers delicious results.

HOW COLD SMOKING WORKS

Food (more specifically meat) is usually cured before smoking, as the curing process draws out the moisture that bacteria need in order to grow, and this promotes the absorption of the wood smoke. We are after this smoke flavor, but the penetration of the smoke into the food also creates a barrier to pests and bacteria. Very little hardening of the outside surface of the meat or casing occurs in cold smoking, so the smoke penetrates the food easily and completely.

GUIDELINES

- Choose a cool day.
- Monitor the temperature of your smoke.
- Make sure you leave sufficient space around the food for the smoke to circulate.
- Leave smoked food in the fridge for at least 24 hours before eating (wrap it well).
- Make sure your sawdust or wood chippings have not been contaminated by unwanted types of wood.
- Put your food in the smoker when it is operational and producing lots of smoke.

THE RIGHT TEMPERATURE

Cold smoking is a bit trickier than hot smoking, because it's important that the smoking temperature is under 20°C (68°F). With a little care this is achievable, but it usually means that any heat source used to get the wood product to smoulder must be kept separate from the smoking chamber. If you get this wrong, the food can start to cook and will lose its preserving qualities. Higher temperatures will also provide exactly the conditions in which bacteria thrive.

WOOD

It may seem self-evident, but different types of wood will give you different flavors (see page 101 for a selection of our favorites). There are some woods to avoid, specifically softwoods such as pine or fir, as their high resin and tar content will spoil the taste of your food. As a rule of thumb, temperate hardwoods are what you need.

SOURCING YOUR WOOD

You have to be careful when sourcing your wood – it's not quite as simple as visiting a local carpenter or joiner who makes lovely wooden furniture and getting an endless supply of shavings and sawdust. Many workshops use a variety of different materials, and a bag of shavings contaminated by softwood or the dust from MDF will render

Cold smoking needs little equipment, just good products

your food inedible and dangerous. So make sure you explain exactly what you need. Of course, you can also collect your own wood and pass it through a chipper. Autumn and winter are probably the best times to do this, when there is less sap in the wood.

BURNING

How you arrange your wood in your smoker will determine how long it will burn, the density of the smoke and the heat, all of which are important to control.

We start by laying a trail of sawdust in the bottom of our oil-drum smoker, making a horse-shoe shape – about 15 cm (6 inches) high and wide – up against the wall of the drum. We use sawdust as it does not burst into

flames as easily as wood shavings; that said, it can be difficult to light. We use a blowtorch, held in place for about 30 seconds or until there is a glowing ember, to light one end of the trail and then allow the sawdust to burn around the ring. You can expect a trail of sawdust that reaches halfway around the drum to burn for about 8 hours. Three-quarters of the drum circumference should last 12 hours, so it will burn through the night. The burning time will be shorter if there are significant drafts or if you use a light sawdust like ash.

If you have a separate smoke box you can use wood shavings or chippings, which tend to burn at a higher temperature than sawdust. The shavings can ignite if you are not careful, which will greatly reduce the smoking time

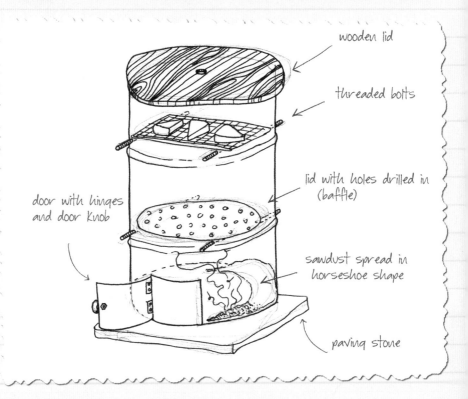

wooden lid

threaded bolts

lid with holes drilled in (baffle)

door with hinges and door knob

sawdust spread in horseshoe shape

paving stone

and smoke density. The more compacted the shavings are, the slower they will burn.

USING YOUR COLD-SMOKER

Your cold-smoker will hold a significant amount of product, and you should use it to its full capacity whenever possible. When your fill the smoker, make sure to leave space for the smoke to circulate. To keep different products in the smoker from tainting each other, you also need to make sure that they are far enough apart – you don't want your cheese to be affected by a fish in close proximity to it.

SAFETY!

When you are smoking meat or fish it is important that the temperature you keep the food at is out of the range that is ideal for bacterial growth. The really dangerous area is near our body temperature, as that is when bacteria thrive and grow very quickly. As a rule of thumb, never cook food in temperatures between 25°C and 60°C (75–140°F).

COLD SMOKING FOOD

PRODUCT	COMMENTS	TIME
Cheese	Cut into pieces weighing about 500 g (1 pound); you can do a lot at one time.	6–8 hours
Ham	After curing, rinse, dry and place in the smoker with lots of room around it.	24–48 hours
Bacon	See pages 142–143.	
Salami (before air drying)	Place in the smoker. After smoking, allow it to hang in order to mature (very light smoke flavor).	4–8 hours
Salami (after air drying)	After air-drying, smoke, keep for 24 hours, then eat.	4–8 hours
Nuts	Arrange in a single layer on a tray.	4 hours
Garlic	Space the bulbs apart on a rack.	6 hours
Salmon	See pages 146–147.	
Whole trout	Gut the fish, cure for about 2–3 hours, dry, then either put a twig through the eye sockets and hang it vertically or lay it on a rack.	4–6 hours
Eggs	Shelled hard-boiled eggs are magnificent when lightly smoked.	2 hours

COLD-SMOKED BACON

Once you've learned how to make your own bacon (see pages 46-47), it's a natural progression to want to smoke it. Bacon can be made from lots of different cuts of pork, and the way the meat is cured and smoked can create subtle differences in flavor. Lean Canadian (back) bacon, which comes from the cured loin, is one of the most popular types of bacon, and side bacon (regular bacon made pork belly) is an economic option, but it is also worth considering the subtlety of collar bacon and remembering that side bacon has lots of culinary uses. Just as the cuts and cures are infinitely variable, so too are the possible ways of smoking it. Different woods will make the bacon taste different, and the smoking time will also have a huge effect on the finished product.

CHOOSING A CUT

The most popular cut of pork for bacon used to be the boned and rolled collar joint that comes from the shoulder area just behind the head of the pig. It used to be a family favorite. The "prime collar" weighs about 2.5 kg (5½ pounds) and the smaller "end collar" weighs about 1 kg (2 pounds). There is also the "fore hock," the front leg of the pig, which can be divided into the "prime hock," which is a bit on the fatty side but adds amazing flavor to soups and stews of dried peas and lentils, and the "hock knuckle," the meat of which is excellent in stews and casseroles.

If you want to be a bit adventurous, ask your butcher for a boned piece of pork that has the loin and the belly in one. It takes moments to prepare, and you then have the ability to taste both smoked Canadian bacon and smoked regular side bacon at the end of the process.

If you want to start with something simpler, try a piece of belly for regular side bacon or loin if you want to make Canadian bacon.

CURING THE MEAT

First you need to cure your bacon. Your decision is whether to dry-cure (see pages 42–45) or to brine (see page 18–21). Both methods will work, but if you are attempting

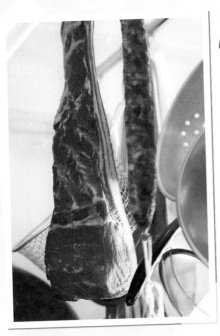

Just hang the bacon up if you're going to eat it in a matter of days

to suggest what type of sawdust to start with, as they all have unique flavors. Oak or apple smoked bacon is what many people expect, but it may be worth experimenting with something like beech for your first batch. Over time it is also worth trying to source maple, mesquite and hickory to smoke your bacon.

SMOKING THE MEAT

The bacon can be placed in the smoker on a rack or hung from a special bacon hanger or even a meat hook. Check the temperature and monitor the smoker occasionally to make sure it remains lit. Smoke the bacon for approximately 8 hours or until you are happy with the color.

FINISHING IT OFF

When you are satisfied with the smoked bacon, take it out of the smoker, wrap it in parchment paper or foil, and store it in the fridge for 24 hours to allow the flavor to permeate the meat fully. The bacon can be kept in the fridge for a couple of weeks if it is kept wrapped up.

SERVING IT UP

Once the bacon is ready to use, slice it up and away you go. Put your slice of bacon into a frying pan without any oil. Place on the heat, and as it heats up the bacon will render enough fat to cook it efficiently.

Regular side bacon is particularly good diced and can be used in numerous dishes. Large cuts of smoked bacon are magnificent, boiled and served hot or cold. They are especially good served hot with parsley sauce.

this for the first time, a simple dry cure using a plastic container with a couple of drainage holes in the bottom and a lid is the easiest method. Keep the cure simple, as the flavor should really come from the smoke.

DRYING THE MEAT

Remove the bacon from the cure, rinse it well and pat it dry with papertowels. Hang it in a cool, dry place for about 1 hour. When drying is complete, a dried salt/sugar coating will be left on the flesh (this is called a pellicle). This coating will help the bacon take the smoke much more effectively. The meat needs to be well dried so that it will color evenly and have an even amount of smoke throughout.

PREPARING THE SMOKER

Light your smoker and allow it to reach a steady state of smoke production. It is hard

A classic bacon sandwich for breakfast is difficult to beat. It's also true that the better the bacon, the better the sandwich. We both love home-smoked bacon, and this BLT is the perfect way to enjoy it.

Serves 2

2 small ciabatta rolls (but any bread will do)

a little olive oil

6 slices smoked bacon

2 garlic cloves

60 ml (¼ cup) mayonnaise

2 large ripe tomatoes

2 handfuls mixed salad leaves

For the guacamole

1 ripe avocado

15 ml (1 tablespoon) chopped fresh cilantro

juice of ½ lime

½ mild red chili

½ red onion, diced

salt and freshly ground black pepper

THE ULTIMATE BLT

Cut your ciabatta rolls in half lengthways and toast them on both sides until golden.

While the rolls are toasting, heat a drop of oil in a pan. Add the bacon and fry until cooked to your preference. Remove the bacon from the pan and keep it warm.

Next, make the guacamole by spooning out the avocado flesh and chopping it roughly with the cilantro, lime juice, chili and red onion. Season with salt and pepper.

Finely chop the garlic and mix it with the mayonnaise in a small bowl. Spread the mayonnaise mixture over the bread and put under the grill for a couple of minutes.

Slice the tomatoes into large circular disks and then plate up your BLT. Start by layering salad leaves on top of the warm garlic mayonnaise and placing tomato slices on top. Next add the bacon and a generous dollop of guacamole.

The thinner the slices, the better

COLD-SMOKED SALMON

The difference between hot-smoked and cold-smoked salmon is that the hot-smoked variety is fully cooked (with a flaky texture), while cold-smoked salmon remains silky and firm. Cold smoking also leads to more flavorful fish, as the smoke penetrates more easily. It's fantastically simple to make.

PREPARING THE SALMON

First you need to prepare the salmon for curing. You will need a fillet with the skin left on. Either fillet it yourself (see pages 54–55) or buy it already filleted. Check for pin bones and remove any that remain.

CURING THE FILLET

Put a layer of salt/sugar mix (see page 56) in the bottom of a dish and add the salmon, skin side down. Rub the flesh side with more of the mixture, then spread about 2–3 mm (about ¼ inch) of the cure over the fish and put it in the fridge for about 4 hours. Rinse off the cure, dry very well with papertowels, then leave to air-dry for at least 12 hours.

PREPARING THE SMOKER

Until you are experienced in smoking your own salmon, always start with less smoke than you think is necessary. It's surprising how much flavor there is in even a lightly colored piece of salmon. Choose the sawdust you wish to use (if in doubt, use oak). Put sufficient sawdust into your smoke box and light it, allowing the smoker to fill with dense smoke.

SMOKING THE SALMON

Put the salmon into the smoker and put the lid on. Monitor the temperature and check to make sure you continue to generate smoke. If you cannot keep your smoker alight, increase the air flow. Remember to take any food out before you relight the smoker because the ash will land on the food.

FINISHING IT OFF

After about 4 hours' smoking time (and a maximum of 6 hours), take the salmon out, wrap it in parchment paper or foil and store in the fridge to allow the flavor to fully permeate the fish. After 24 hours, enjoy. The salmon will keep in the fridge for 2–3 weeks.

NOW TRY: TROUT

Gut the fish and remove the gills, rub the inside thoroughly with the cure, then coat with the rest of the mix and cure for 2–3 hours. Rinse, pat dry with papertowels, then allow the fish to air-dry for at least 8 hours. Put them into the smoker for 4 hours, either on a rack or with a twig through the eye sockets so that you can hang them up.

HOW TO COLD-SMOKE SALMON

Start by filleting your salmon and removing any pin bones that remain.

Cure the fish for about 4 hours. Then rinse off the cure and dry with papertowels.

Put sufficient sawdust into your smoke box and light it, allowing the smoker to fill with dense smoke. Put the salmon into the box, put the lid on and smoke for 4–6 hours.

Remove the salmon from the smoker, wrap it in parchment paper or foil and store in the fridge to allow the flavor to fully permeate the fish.

Blini are little pancakes made from a yeasted batter that is traditionally made with buckwheat flour. They are the perfect base for a canapé and can be topped with any number of ingredients. Here we've gone for the delicious combination of crème fraîche, smoked salamon and caviar. If you don't have a blini pan, a heavy frying pan will do.

Makes about 25

100 g (3½ ounces) smoked salmon, cut into strips

1 small tub crème fraîche or sour cream

1 jar lumpfish caviar

For the blini

50 g (2 ounces) buckwheat flour (about 75 ml/ ⅓ cup)

150 g (5 ounces) white flour (about 310 ml/ 1¼ cups)

5 ml (1 teaspoon) salt

1 (7 g/¼-ounce) package fast-acting yeast

2 eggs, separated

310 ml (1¼ cups) milk, warmed

clarified butter, for cooking

SMOKED SALMON BLINI

To make the blini, sift both the flours into a bowl and add the salt and yeast. Beat the egg yolks in a second bowl and add the warm milk. Pour the yolk and milk mixture into the flour mixture and mix until just combined. Cover the bowl with a tea towel and set aside for about 1 hour, until the yeast gets active and the mixture looks spongy.

Whisk the egg whites to stiff peaks and carefully fold into the batter with a metal spoon, trying to keep the mixture as airy as possible. Let the mixture stand for at least 15 minutes.

Put your blini pan or heavy frying pan on medium heat, and when it's hot add a little oil or clarified butter. Drop spoonfuls of the batter into the pan. They take about 1½ minutes per side to cook. Repeat until you have used all the mixture.

When you've made your blini, you can assemble them. Start with a layer of crème fraîche or sour cream, then add a layer of smoked salmon and top with caviar.

Tiny, fluffy blini are a treat

As a treat for Sunday breakfast or a light lunch, this is a simple dish that gives the illusion of decadence yet is very good value. When we travel around we rate hotels by the quality of their scrambled eggs -- everyone can make them, but too often they are dry and over-cooked. For us they have to be rich, soft and very creamy.

Serves 4

8 free-range eggs

salt and freshly ground black pepper

50 g (2 ounces) smoked salmon

75 g (3 ounces) butter (about 75 ml/⅓ cup)

15 ml (1 tablespoon) chopped fresh dill

4 thick slices of whole-grain bread, toasted

SMOKED SALMON WITH SCRAMBLED EGGS

Beat the eggs well and add a pinch of salt. Cut the smoked salmon into small pieces about 5×5mm (¼ × ¼ inch).

Melt about 50 g (2 ounces) of the butter (about 45 ml/3 tablespoons) in a nonstick pan, then pour in the beaten eggs and stir slowly while they cook. The eggs will start to firm up. While they are still soft, take them off the heat, add the remaining butter and stir it in briskly. From here on speed is of the essence, as no more heat will be added and the dish will start to cool.

Stir in the salmon and the dill until evenly distributed. Pop the eggs on to the toast and serve with a crack of black pepper.

Smoked salmon has long been considered a luxury and is often only bought for special occasions. Having the ability to smoke your own salmon makes this a reasonably cheap dish, yet it is flavorful and rich.

Serves 4

olive oil

500 g (1 pound) linguine or spaghetti

1 garlic clove, chopped

200 g (7 ounces) smoked salmon, cut into small pieces

1 handful fresh dill, finely chopped

15 ml (1 tablespoon) lemon juice

250 ml (1 cup) heavy cream (36%)

salt and freshly ground black pepper

PASTA WITH SMOKED SALMON

Bring a large pan of salted water to a boil and add a drizzle of olive oil. Add the pasta and cook so it is still quite firm, being careful not to overcook it.

While the pasta is cooking, heat 15 ml (1 tablespoon) of olive oil in a frying pan and add the garlic. Cook gently until softened, and then add the smoked salmon, dill, lemon juice and cream. Heat through and season with salt and pepper to taste.

When the pasta is ready, strain it, reserving the cooking water. Add the pasta to the frying pan and stir gently, adding a little of the cooking water if necessary to loosen the texture. Serve.

Fish cakes are very popular in our household, and our fish cake recipe results in a lumpy fusion of spicy, piquant flavors. If you want to try something different, you could use smoked haddock or cod instead of the salmon.

Serves 4

1 kg (2 pounds) new potatoes

150 g (5 ounces) smoked salmon, roughly chopped

4 spring onions, roughly sliced

2 fresh red chilies, chopped into rings, seeds and all

100 g (3½ ounces) pitted black or green olives, roughly chopped

15 ml (1 tablespoon) capers, roughly chopped

½ egg, beaten

45 ml (3 tablespoons) roughly chopped fresh cilantro

juice and zest of ½ lime

30 ml (2 tablespoons) flour

salt and freshly ground black pepper

extra virgin olive oil

For the lime mayonnaise

juice and zest of ½ lime

1 garlic clove, crushed

60 ml (¼ cup) mayonnaise

To serve

sweet chili dipping sauce

SMOKED SALMON FISH CAKES

Bring a large pan of salted water to a boil and add the potatoes. Cook until tender, and then crush roughly, leaving some small chunks and some larger ones. Set aside to cool.

Put the potatoes, salmon, spring onions, chilies, olives, capers, egg and cilantro in a large bowl. Add the lime zest and juice and mix thoroughly. Sprinkle the flour over and mix it in. Season with salt and pepper. Take handfuls of the mixture, form them into balls, and place them on a baking sheet. They can be kept for several hours in the fridge at this stage if necessary.

Heat a good splash of extra virgin olive oil in your frying pan. Add your balls of fish mixture, spacing generously. Once you have your pan full, gently press the balls flat with a fish spatula or regular spatula.

Give the pan a gentle shake to make sure the fish cakes have not stuck, and then leave them until the first side is golden brown – about 5 minutes, depending on the heat. Turn carefully and cook the other side.

To make the lime mayonnaise, mix together all the ingredients in a small bowl.

Serve the fish cakes with a green salad, the lime mayonnaise and a sweet chili dipping sauce.

KIPPERS

A kipper is a herring that has been cold smoked. If the herring is not gutted before smoking, it is referred to as a bloater and the flavor is somewhat "gamier." Other oily fish such as mackerel can be treated in similar ways to herring.

CREATING KIPPERS

To make kippers, first you must to fillet your herring. You need to cure the fish for 30 minutes and then rinse and dry the fillets before putting them your smoke box for 6–8 hours. After the smoking, take the kippers out, wrap them in parchment paper or foil and store in the fridge for up to 1 week.

SERVING IT UP

To cook the kippers, place them skin side down on a grill pan. Smear them with a knob of butter and grill under high heat for about 4 minutes.

Lay the herring on its belly on a board. Slice along the backbone, through the head and into the body cavity, taking care not to cut through the stomach.

Put the herrings in a dish and cover with a salt/sugar cure for 30 minutes – 75 g (3 ounces) salt (about 75 ml/$^1/_3$ cup) and 25g (1 ounce) sugar (about about 30 ml/ 2 tablespoons) will do a couple of herrings easily.

Use papertowels to pull out all the guts.

Turn the fish over, press flat and pop out the eyeballs (so that you can pop a stick through the sockets when the fish is hung up to smoke).

Rinse, dry with papertowels then air-dry for a couple of hours. Once the herring are dry, put sufficient sawdust into your smoke box and light it, allowing the smoker to fill with dense smoke.

Put the herrings in the smoker and put the lid on. Monitor the temperature and check that you continue to generate smoke. In 6–8 hours you'll have kippers.

Kedgeree is a classic English breakfast dish that we don't eat often enough in North America. There are dozens of variations on this mildly curried smoked fish dish, but we like to serve it with a whole kipper and a poached egg on top.

Serves 4

50g (2 ounces) butter (about 45 mL/3 tablespoons)

4 kippers

salt and freshly ground black pepper

500 ml (2 cups) chicken stock

200 g (7 ounces) basmati rice (about 250 mL/1 cup)

4 large fresh eggs

1 onion, diced

15 ml (1 tablespoon) medium curry powder or paste

2 ml (½ teaspoon) turmeric

1 red pepper, diced

30 ml (2 tablespoons) roughly chopped fresh flat leaf parsley

GRILLED KIPPER KEDGEREE WITH POACHED EGG

Smear half the butter equally over the inside of each of the kippers. Grind a little black pepper over the butter. Place the kippers, skin side down, in a grill pan and cook under a hot grill for about 4 minutes, or until cooked through.

Bring the stock to a boil in a large pan. Rinse the rice under cold running water, and then add to the stock and cook for about 10 minutes or until the rice is tender. Drain, but do not rinse.

While the rice is cooking, soft poach the eggs and keep warm.

Melt the remaining butter in a large sauté pan or wok, then add the onion and cook gently until softened. Add the curry powder and turmeric and cook for 2 minutes more. Add the red pepper and cook for another 3 minutes, then add the cooked rice and mix well. Take off the heat and stir in the parsley.

Serve with a kipper and a poached egg on top.

COLD-SMOKED CHEESE

There are more and more artisan cheesemakers these days, producing tasty and unique products. In fact, they all make something a bit different, which is what they have in common. You may not yet be ready to enter the cheese-makers' world of rennet, curds and whey, but you too can create your own cheese product by smoking your favorite variety. Smoked cheese is heavily dependent on the type of wood that you use, and different flavors will work with different cheeses -- the matching up is completely down to personal taste, so give it a try and work out your favorite combination. You can use the same technique to cold-smoke eggs and cod roe.

PREPARING THE CHEESE

Many cheeses work well when smoked, but the best for beginners are harder varieties such as cheddar, Stilton and Gouda. Each of these has its own qualities that work in unusual ways with the smoked flavors. Have fun and don't overdo it – sometimes the tastiest smoked cheese is one that is hard to distinguish from the original. Cut your cheese into large chunks rather than individual slices. Ideally, you want individual segments weighing about 200 g (7 ounces) each.

SMOKING YOUR CHEESE

Position the chunks of cheese on a rack so they are not touching – you want smoke to be able to circulate freely around the smoker and reach all parts of the cheese.

Place the cheese in your smoker towards the top of the chamber, away from any direct heat. If it is too hot, the cheese will melt and drip through the wire mesh, which is very messy! Cold-smoke for 4–5 hours, using oak, beech or apple sawdust.

FINISHING IT OFF

The best way to enjoy your smoked cheese is to leave it in the fridge, wrapped in foil or parchment paper, for at least 24 hours before eating. It should keep for at least 2–3 weeks.

NOW TRY: EGGS

Once you get into smoking food you automatically join a secret society of other fans of this cooking style. People will swap stories with you, share tips and exchange secret recipes at the drop of a hat. Our secret is smoked eggs! Take a hard-boiled egg and smoke it as you would cheese for 1–2 hours. The smoke will gradually penetrate to the yolk and provide you with a delicious snack. Perfect served as a gourmet egg salad sandwich with homemade mayonnaise, a pinch of smoked paprika and some cress.

NOW TRY: COD ROE

A pressed slice of cod roe is delicious when cold smoked. It adds an earthy undulation to the fishy taste. The roe can be grated to add a smoky, fishy flavor to other fish dishes or sauces and is outstanding as the basis for a rather unusual taramosalata. Try blending with garlic, salt and olive oil prior to adding to mashed potatoes for fish pie.

Pop the food in the smoker

This recipe uses smoked eggs and spicy chorizo to create a unique snack that is perfect to take on picnics. For a different flavor combination, use plain sausage meat and blend it with parsley, spring onions and orange zest before wrapping up the egg.

Makes 8

500 g (1 pound) fresh chorizo sausages

250 g (9 ounces) flour (about 500 ml/2 cups)

sea salt and freshly ground black pepper

8 smoked eggs

250 g (9 ounces) bread crumbs (about 500 ml/2 cups)

zest of 1 lemon

10 ml (2 teaspoons) fresh thyme leaves

2 eggs, beaten

vegetable oil, for deep-frying

SMOKED SCOTCH EGG

Squeeze the chorizo meat out of the sausage casings and divide into eight balls. Using a rolling pin and working on a floured surface, roll each ball into an oval shape about 12 cm (5 inches) long by 8 cm (3 inches) across at its widest point and lay them out on a board or other work surface.

Season the flour with salt and pepper and put it in a shallow bowl. Coat the smoked eggs in the seasoned flour and place one on top of each oval chorizo disk.

Bring the edges of the sausage meat up around each egg so they are completely covered then form them into oval balls.

Put the bread crumbs in a bowl and mix in the lemon zest, thyme leaves and a pinch of sea salt. Put the beaten eggs in a shallow dish. Dip each ball into the beaten egg then roll in the bread crumbs.

Heat the vegetable oil for deep-frying in a large pan. Add the Scotch eggs, two at a time, and deep-fry for 8–10 minutes or until golden brown.

This easy recipe shows off smoked Stilton beautifully, and we like to add buttery leeks and walnuts to complement the cheese. Serve the tart with a fresh salad and some sweet cherry tomatoes to cut through the creamy texture.

Serves 4

20g (¾ ounces) butter (about 22 ml/1½ tablespoons), plus a little for greasing

1 leek, finely chopped

5 ml (1 teaspoon) lemon juice

250ml (1 cup) milk

1 egg, beaten

100 g (3½ ounces) cheddar cheese, grated

salt and freshly ground black pepper

450 g (15½ ounces) shortcrust pastry

50 g (2 ounces) walnuts, chopped

200 g (7 ounces) smoked Stilton cheese, roughly diced

SMOKED STILTON TART

Preheat the oven to 180°C (350°F), and grease a 20 cm (8-inch) flan pan.

Melt the butter in a pan and add the leeks and lemon juice. Cook gently until softened then set aside to cool.

Put the milk in a bowl and mix in the beaten egg and grated cheese. Season with salt and pepper.

Roll out the pastry on a floured surface until you have a circle about 5 mm (¼ inch) thick. Lay the pastry in the dish and use a fork to prick it in a few places. Put a piece of parchment paper over the pastry, spread a layer of dried beans on top, then put it in the oven and blind bake for 12 minutes. Remove from the oven and discard the beans and paper.

Spread the leeks, walnuts and smoked Stilton in the pastry case and pour over the milk and egg mixture. Put back into the oven and bake for a further 15 minutes, until golden.

Stuffed jalapeños are a treat when served with a big Mexican-style meal or as an appetizer. We love this version with smoked Gouda cheese. These poppers are best made the night before and left in the freezer until you need them for your fiesta.

Serves 4

2 chorizo sausages, finely diced

2 red onions, finely diced

500 g (1 pound) smoked Gouda cheese, grated

100 g (3½ ounces) cream cheese

24 jalapeño chilies

100 g (3½ ounces) bread crumbs

5 ml (1 teaspoon) paprika

salt and freshly ground black pepper

60 ml (¼ cup) flour

2 eggs, beaten

vegetable oil, for deep-frying

To serve

sour cream

SMOKED CHEESE & JALAPEÑO POPPERS

Put the diced chorizo and red onions in a bowl with the smoked Gouda and cream cheese. Mix together well.

Slice the jalapeños in half lengthways and remove the seeds. Use a teaspoon to fill the jalapeños with the chorizo and cheese mixture, and then press the halves together to re-form the whole jalapeños. Set aside.

Put the bread crumbs in a shallow bowl and mix with the paprika and a good pinch of salt and pepper. Pour the eggs into a shallow dish. Put the flour on a small plate and line up the bread crumbs and beaten eggs alongside. Dip the jalapeños into the flour, shaking off the excess, then dip them into the beaten egg and finally into the bread crumbs.

Place the stuffed jalapeños on a baking sheet and put in the freezer for 2 hours. Cook right from the freezer when ready. Drop them into hot oil and deep-fry for 3 minutes or until golden brown, and then place them on papertowels to drain off the excess oil.

Serve with sour cream.

If you've never eaten cod's roe before, you really must give it a try. We like to shallow-fry it to retain the delicate smoky flavor. The other advantage of this way of cooking cod's roe is that it is crispy on the outside and soft in the middle. A quick cream and mustard sauce brings this dish together -- the mustard perfectly complementing the smoky cod's roe.

Serves 1

1 spring onion, finely chopped

15 ml (1 tablespoon) white wine

5 ml (1 teaspoon) whole-grain mustard

60 ml (¼ cup) heavy cream (36%)

zest of 1 lemon

15 ml (1 tablespoon) chopped fresh flat leaf parsley

15 ml (1 tablespoon) flour

salt and freshly ground black pepper

15-30 ml (1-2 tablespoons) vegetable oil

3 slices of smoked cod's roe, about 1 cm (½ inch) thick

1-2 thick slices of bread, for toasting

SMOKED COD'S ROE WITH A CREAMY MUSTARD SAUCE

To make the sauce, soften the spring onion in the white wine in a pan over moderate heat. When the wine starts to reduce, add the mustard, cream, most of the lemon zest and half the parsley. Bring to a boil, then reduce the heat and simmer for a further minute.

Put the flour in a bowl and season with salt and pepper. Heat the oil in a frying pan. Dip the slices of cod's roe into the flour. Put them straight into the hot oil and fry for 2 minutes on each side. Remove from the pan and blot off any excess oil with papertowels.

Make the toast, top with cod's roe and pour the sauce over. Garnish with the remaining parsley and lemon zest and serve.

INDEX

ACKNOWLEDGMENTS

PICTURE CREDITS

All photographs © **Nick Pope** with the exception of the following: **Fotolia**/Monica Butnaru (used throughout). **Strawbridge Family Archive** 19 (top left), 20 (top left and right), 43 (top and bottom right), 44 (bottom left), 63 (bottom), 69 (bottom left and right), 70 (right), 99 (bottom left), 139 (bottom left and right). **Thinkstock**/iStockphoto (used throughout).

Illustrations: **Charlotte Strawbridge** 16, 40, 66, 96, 136. **James Strawbridge** 18, 57, 70, 103, 106, 107, 140.

Publisher: Stephanie Jackson
Managing Editor: Clare Churly
Copy-editor: Annie Lee
Creative Director: Jonathan Christie
Designer: Jaz Bahra
Illustrators: Charlotte Strawbridge, James Strawbridge
Photographer: Nick Pope
Stylist: Alison Clarkson
Kitchen Dogsbody: Jim Tomson
Production Manager: Pete Hunt